To and from

CRACK

to Christ

A Sinner in Recovery

ANONYMOUS SINNER

ISBN 978-1-64191-162-7 (paperback)
ISBN 978-1-64191-163-4 (digital)

Christian Faith Publishing, Inc.
832 Park Avenue
Meadville, PA 16335
www.christianfaithpublishing.com

Unless otherwise noted: Scripture quotations are taken from the Holy Bible, New Living Translation, copyright 1996. Used by permission of Tyndale House Publishers, Inc., Carol Stream, Illinois 60188. All rights reserved.

Other scriptures are taken from the King James Version and the AV7.

The 12 Step quotations are taken from the Narcotics Anonymous (NA) fifth edition.

"Reprinted by permission of NA World Services, Inc. All rights reserved. The Twelve Steps of NA reprinted for adaptation by permission of AA World Services, Inc."

I would like to dedicate this testimony to God for sending His Son to pay for my deliverance from my addictions. It is only by His stripes that I am healed.

I thank God for my mother, who taught me as a child about God's love for me. Without her teaching me, I would not have known to call on Jesus in my time of need.

I also would like to thank my family for their continued love and support during the changing of my mind-set.

To my daughter, I love you, and I thank God and you for forgiving me for my past mistakes and for accepting me as the sinner in recovery that I am.

IF I HAVE TO, I'LL PRAISE ALONE

I'm not a preacher or a minister, but I am a sinner in recovery and a testifier. This book is only part of my testimony because I am still a work in progress. You may or may not completely understand why I testify and give God praise because the challenges I've faced have been different than the one's you've had.

Today, I praise God for my deliverance from drugs and alcohol. I praise Him because when it's cold outside I have a warm place to lay my head. During the last few years of my addictions, I was living in a vacant building.

I praise Him for giving me the mind to start my website Anonymous Sinner.com. I pray that it will be a blessing to others the way that it has been a blessing to me. I started the website with the idea that we are all sinners. Although some of my sins may be different from yours, I believe we all have some things in common.

God loves each of us, and we all want to be forgiven for our mistakes. I also believe that God wants us to share some of our struggles with others so that someone can learn from our mistakes while also learning about the grace of God.

Another reason for the website is that I realize that everyone may not be comfortable with public speaking or sharing things that are personal, even though sometimes sharing can help ease the stress from a difficult situation.

I give praise because at the age of twelve I started slipping into a world of addictions that lasted until the age of forty-two. Though some may disagree with me because of what someone else has said in the past, I no longer call myself an addict because I no longer do the things I used to do.

I do, however, consider myself to be a sinner in recovery because I still have free will to make good or bad decisions, and will for as long as I live. I also have a chance to recover from my mistakes by learning from them, asking for forgiveness, and sharing what I've experienced in hopes that others can relate to them and, in some cases, avoid making some of the same mistakes.

I give praise for sometimes being able to pray for others and offer encouragement because I appreciate all the prayers that were made on my behalf. I praise God in spite of the situations that will arrive with the understanding that no matter what happens having just one hit will hurt; therefore, I will not use my free will to make that bad decision.

I give God praise because He's worthy to be praised and for giving me the understanding that everyone is a sinner, but everyone is not comfortable speaking in front of others. Therefore, I would like to invite you to join me as a sinner in recovery in giving God praise and sharing what you are going through, and some of the things that you have made it through because of God's grace at www. AnonymousSinner.com.

You're invited, but if I have to, I'll praise alone.

God bless you.

TO AND FROM CRACK TO CHRIST

A SINNER IN RECOVERY

I am a sinner seeking the kingdom of heaven. Though I continue to make mistakes, I pray for forgiveness, a better understanding of God's Word, and that through Christ my soul will be recovered when my Savior (Christ) returns. I AM A SINNER IN RECOVERY.

WARNING!

THE DEVIL IS A LIAR! He does not have your best interests in mind. His only goal is to get you to dishonor God and to see you in HELL! Only you can stop him from achieving his goal by accepting Christ as your savior and taking the time to develop a personal relationship with God. YOUR DESTINY AND SOUL ARE AT RISK!

HOW STRONG ARE YOU
SPIRITUALLY?

"Is your life worth fighting for?" What kind of question is that to ask someone? If you ask, would you expect an answer other than yes? Everyone has a natural fight-or-flight instinct, and to keep oneself from harm, it kicks in automatically without thought. If at any time you are in a situation where there's no escape and you are forced to fight to protect yourself from being hurt, you will fight.

Most people will not just lie down and take a beating. They will try to swing, kick, or bite their way out of the situation. We do all this for a temporary body that will eventually fail us one day. No matter how good a fighter you are, you will eventually lose your fight to keep yourself here physically. For just as each of us are born physically, so will we one day die physically.

Out of all the time we spend fighting for our temporary physical lives through dieting, exercising, taking boxing or karate classes, or learning to shoot a gun, how much time have YOU invested in protecting YOUR spiritual life, which is ETERNAL? When was the last time you exercised your mind and soul to strengthen your spiritual life? Are you the type to do something physical every day and do something spiritual once a week, or maybe just on Easter and Christmas?

How strong are you spiritually, because your spiritual strength will determine the outcome of your most important fight? The fight for your soul's eternity. Just like we feed our bodies every day so that our bodies will be strong, we must also get into the habit of feeding our minds and souls. The Bible tells us that "people need more than bread for their life; they must feed on every word of God" (Matthew 4:4).

When was the last time you fed your soul? Aren't you hungry? Are your spiritual ribs showing? FEED YOURSELF! You don't have to try to eat the full meal all at once, but it is vital to your eternal soul that you eat something daily. You can start feeding your soul by simply changing the CD you're listening to. Instead of listening to some R & B, rap, pop, or country, try listening to some gospel. We all have our own faults, most of which can be changed by the grace of God through prayer and by changing our mind-sets.

Your mind-set can only be changed by changing some of what you watch, read, and listen to; changing the places you go and the people whom you socialize with; STUDYING GOD'S WORD; and, most of all, taking time to develop a personal relationship with Him.

As you continue to study God's Word, your soul will continue to be fed. As you continue to feed your soul, your spiritual strength will increase. It is a process of strength building that just doesn't happen overnight; you have to keep at it for yourself. The world's strongest man was not born that way. He went through the process of strength training for his body.

For us to build our spiritual strength, we need to go through the process of spiritual training by going to church, accepting Christ as our savior, studying the Word, and feeding our souls daily. GOD IS GOOD! He has made it so that we do not have to go to church every day. We can read our Bibles in the comfort of our homes, listen to gospel radio or CDs, and even turn on the TV or get on the Internet and find a gospel program or website.

Even in times when none of those sources are available, we all still have a direct line to our Father in heaven through our Savior Jesus. God is everywhere, and when we can't sit down to study the Word, we can always ask our Father to send us a word and pray that our eyes and ears are opened to receive and understand it when it comes.

It's easy for us to feed our spirits somehow on a daily basis, but first, we must realize and come to understand what that empty feeling is that we feel inside. That empty feeling that we have is a void in our lives that can only be filled by God and His Word. Until we use our free will to seek Him, it will remain empty, or maybe just not full enough, and our spirits will remain weak. Start or revive your spiritual strength training today. Your eternal soul depends on it.

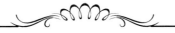

A DECEPTION

One of the devil's greatest deceptions was to convince people that he didn't exist. This has made it much easier for him to steal souls from people who are unaware of his presence and his intents. The devil's main purpose is to dishonor God and to get others to do the same.

The devil knows his future is in hell, and he wants to take as many souls with him as possible. I guess that's where the world gets that "If I'm going down, I'm taking you with me" attitude. He seeks those who are not fully aware of his presence or the power that they have through Christ. Once he finds a soul that doesn't realize the potential that was given to them on Calvary, he finds ways to break them down, keep them down, and take their focus off God.

Many people who are unaware of the devil's presence dishonor God on a regular basis by not taking time to seek Him and study His Word for themselves (some even believe in God and the devil). We sometimes get so relaxed and attached to things of the world that we dishonor God by ignoring Him and His Word, even though He's always in the same room with us.

Now the devil has used deception to convinced millions of people that they suffer from a disease for which there's no cure (the disease of addictions), when the Bible (God's Word) clearly states that **"through Christ all things are possible and that by His (Christ Jesus) stripes we are healed" (1 Peter 2:24).**

The devil knows your weakness better than you do, and loves to use them against you. He knows exactly how to push your buttons, and he is counting on YOU not to educate YOURSELF. It's only with the words of the Living God that we can learn how to push back when we can, and learn to let go and let God when we can't.

The devil has used deception to trick society into accepting that it is okay to offer or accept drugs and alcohol as a way to get a party started, or to cope with a situation in which someone may need to be consoled, knowing that a person may just be one step away from becoming an addict or relapsing while, at the same time, taking their focus off God.

The continued custom of partying and drowning out our pains with drugs and alcohol needs to be broken, and the only weapon strong enough to break it is God's Word. Each of us needs to learn to read His Word for ourselves. Only then will we start to find there's an answer for every test (situation) that we encounter, for knowledge is power.

Unfortunately, the man-made 12-step programs are not set up to equip many addicts seeking help with all the knowledge they need to have power over their addictions. That power can only be found through Christ under "God's program."

The more we live, the more we will be tested, so we must take it upon ourselves to study God's Word so that we may find the answers we need when needed. We must also learn to place our problems in God's hands when our test becomes too much for us to handle, and have faith that He will take care of them.

If only there was a way to find and study God's Word. Something that would help man get a better understanding of God's will for us all. Some basic instructions that would cover all aspects of life so that whatever came up, man could find a way to deal with it. Wait a minute, there is something like that already, and it's called the Bible.

The Bible is

B—Basic
I—Instructions
B—Before
L—Leaving
E—Earth.

The Bible, it's not just a book; it is the GOD-STEPS PROGRAM!

It is the most important instruction manual you will ever read, and you don't have to be a super saint to get something from it. It is a must-read for the SINNER IN RECOVERY!

I am an anonymous sinner in recovery, and I USED TO BE AN ADDICT.

God has delivered me from drugs and alcohol; therefore, through Christ I am a new creature. I no longer suffer from a disease in which man has no cure for. My higher power is the only Living God, and He is God alone. He has power over all things, including addictions. I am in no way perfect, but I will give thanks each day for where He is taking me and for where He has brought me from. I know that I am still a sinner in recovery and a work in progress.

To better myself by changing my mind-set, I will continue to study and grow in His Word. I pray that this book will be a blessing to you and that you too will continue to grow in Christ. May your prayers be answered as your faith is increased. Until your prayers are answered, keep pressing on. What God has done for others, He can do for you too.

We all have made mistakes in our past, and will continue to do so as long as we live here on earth. Do not let your past keep you from your future blessings. When you fall due to a mistake, learn to pick yourself up, repent, and keep pressing on.

12: I don't mean to say that I have already achieved these things or that I have already reached perfection! But I keep working toward that day when I will finally be all that Christ Jesus saved me for and wants me to be.

13: No, dear brothers and sisters, I am still not all I should be, but I am focusing all my energies on this one thing: Forgetting the past and looking forward to what lies ahead,

14: I strain to reach the end of the race and receive the prize for which God, through Christ Jesus, is calling us up to heaven.

15: I hope all of you who are mature Christians will agree on these things. If you disagree on some point, I believe God will make it plain to you.

16: But we must be sure to obey the truth we have learned already. (Philippians 3:12–16)

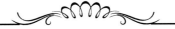

WORDS HAVE POWER

There are three types of words, and they all have power:

1. There's God's words.
2. There's the devil's words.
3. And there's our words.

The power of our words can be increased positively or negatively, depending on who we choose to agree with: God's words or the devil's words. The devil comes to steal, kill, and destroy. The devil has never and never will do anything for your benefit. God sent His Son, Jesus, so that you may have life and have it more abundantly: **"The theif's purpose is to steal and kill and destroy. My purpose is to give life in all its fullness" (John 10:10).**

God tells us in His Word that if we would call on Him that He would answer (**"When they call on me, I will answer; I will be with them in trouble. I will rescue them and honor them" [Psalm 91:15]). That we are more than conquerors (Romans 8:37, KJV), and that by whose stripes ye were healed (1 Peter 2:24, KJV). The Bible also tells us that God is not a man that He should lie (Numbers 23:19).**

So if man lies, the devil comes to destroy, and God never lies. Which words will you choose to agree with? Man's: "Addicts suffer from a disease for which there's no cure," "Once an addict always an addict"? Or God's: **"You are more than a conqueror," "By His stripes you are healed"**?

God gave each of us free will, and we each get to decide for ourselves which words to speak over our lives, whether they be positive or negative. If you or a loved one is struggling with an addiction, find a good church and a 12-step program to attend. Study God's Word for yourself, and pray for a better understanding of it.

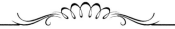

GOING HIGHER THAN 12 STEPS

Finding a good 12-step program is important, but unlike God's program, the 12 steps has its flaws. After all, the 12-step program was developed by man, and only God is perfect. I'm sure that it was not man's intention to deceive millions of people seeking help with addictions, but I'm also sure it was the devil's intention. Twelve-step programs tell the person seeking help that they suffer from a disease for which there's no cure and encourages that person to tell themselves the same. In my opinion, that's one of the reasons why their failure rate is so much higher than their success rate.

Most of the people leaving rehab centers that I have known have relapsed. In my opinion, telling yourself that you will suffer from something for the rest of your life eats away at your hope for your future, and as humans, we all need to feel a since of hope. No one wants to be in and stay in a hopeless situation because it will only break their spirits, and the devil wants your spirit broken. We are all sinners and make mistakes.

God is there for all of us if we would come to Him, ask for forgiveness, and accept Christ as our savior. If we would take it upon ourselves to study His Word, we would see that there's hope for us all even though we remain sinners in recovery.

Think about this for a moment: would you tell your children that they are hopeless, that they would always be hopeless, and encourage them to admit this to themselves and others? Or would you try to educate them while telling them that we all make mistakes but can learn from them and through Christ ALL things are possible and that they could do anything they put their minds to? I believe most people would choose to educate their children.

So why do some people keep telling themselves that they suffer from a disease for which there's no cure, instead of educating themselves by reading the Bible for themselves? Could it be an excuse for sinners in recovery to give up and give in to an addiction when things get hard, or have they been lied to so much that they just accept the lies as truth?

Too many people going through rehab end up relapsing because they just accept what others tell them based on a program designed by man. It is time for an awakening. I have found the 12-step inpatient program to be very beneficial to me when I was recovering from my addictions. (Through Christ I have recovered from addictions, but I'm still a sinner in recovery.)

The program allowed me to speak with counselors as I studied a program that had benefited other addicts. I received a lot of good information. I also realized that the man-made program (the 12-step program) did not always line up with what the Bible (God's program) tells us. It had some truths in it, but there were also things twisted (such as I suffer from a disease for which there's no cure and I will always be an addict). THE DEVIL IS A LIE.

I refuse to believe that God HAS POWER OVER ALL THINGS EXCEPT ADDICTIONS! Through Christ, I have recovered from my addictions, and I am a new creature. That is my faith; what is yours? I thank God for making a way for me to get into rehab and learn about the 12-step program while giving me the mind to study His Word for myself.

I AM AN ANONYMOUS SINNER IN RECOVERY, AND I USE TO BE AN ADDICT!

Some people disagree with my statement "I use to be an addict" because it's not "in line" with what is taught in 12-step programs ("Once an addict, always an addict"), even though some of the people say that they believe in God.

To those people, I say, SHOW ME the scripture that states that addictions is too much for God to handle and then I will call myself an addict. Until then, I'll remain a new creature free from addictions.

(And yes, I am from St. Louis.)

I do not still suffer from the disease of addictions because God has delivered me from that. However, I do still sin. I AM A SINNER IN RECOVERY! I was born a sinner, and will always be a sinner as long as I'm on this earth, and I pray that my soul be recovered when Christ returns.

Through Christ and the studying of the Bible (God's program), I will become better by continuing to seek God and repenting when I'm wrong.

GOD BLESS AMERICA

The United States of America is a country where good men and women have died, and continue to die, in part to protect our freedom of speech, yet many try to remain politically correct in order to avoid conflicts through disagreements. We all, as a human race, need to stop being so politically correct and learn to be more biblically correct!

THE TEN COMMANDMENTS
(EXODUS 20:1–17, KJV [AV7])
(PART OF GOD'S PROGRAM)

1. God spoke saying: I am the Lord your God . . . You shall have no other gods before me.

2. You shall not make for yourself any graven image or any likeness of anything that is in heaven above or that is in the earth beneath or that is in the water under the earth. You shall not bow yourself down to them nor serve them, for I the Lord your God am a jealous God, visiting the iniquity of the fathers upon the children to the third and fourth generation of those who hate me and showing mercy to thousands of those who love me and keep my commandments.

3. You shall not take the name of the Lord your God in vain, for the Lord will not hold those guiltless who take His name in vain.

4. Remember the Sabbath day to keep it holy. Six days shall you labor and do all your work, but the seventh day is the Sabbath of the Lord Your God. In it, you shall not do any work: You nor your son nor your daughter, your servant nor your maid, nor your cattle, nor your visitor who is within your gates.

   For in six days the Lord made heaven and earth, the sea and all that is in them, and He rested on the seventh day. Therefore the Lord blessed the Sabbath day and hallowed it.

5. Honor your father and your mother so that your days may be long upon the land which the Lord your God has given to you.

6. You shall not murder.

7. You shall not commit adultery.

8. You shall not steal.

9. You shall not bear false witness against your neighbor.

10. You shall not covet your neighbor's house, and you shall not covet your neighbor's wife nor his manservant nor his maidservant nor his ox nor his ass nor anything that is your neighbor's.

THE 12 STEPS

1. We admitted that we were powerless over our addiction, that our lives had become unmanageable.
2. We came to believe that a power greater than ourselves could restore us to sanity.
3. We made a decision to turn our will and our lives over to the care of God as we understood Him.
4. We made a searching and fearless moral inventory of ourselves.
5. We admitted to God, to ourselves, and to another human being the exact nature of our wrongs.
6. We were entirely ready to have God remove all these defects of character.
7. We humbly asked Him to remove our shortcomings.
8. We made a list of all persons we had harmed, and became willing to make amends to them all.
9. We made direct amends to such people wherever possible, except when to do so would injure them or others.
10. We continued to take personal inventory and when we were wrong promptly admitted it.
11. We sought through prayer and meditation to improve our conscious contact with God as we understood Him, praying only for knowledge of His will for us and the power to carry that out.
12. Having had a spiritual awakening as a result of these steps, we tried to carry this message to addicts, and to practice these principles in all our affairs.

The 12 steps are a good set of rules to go by for some help as long as we understand that they are words of men, not God's words. Unfortunately, in order to try to please everyone, 12-step programs, in my opinion, are being "politically correct" and they've replaced God with a "higher power," For some, what is this "higher power"? Is it something other than God?

This clearly breaks the first commandment. So many people are seeking the blessing of recovery from addictions, and the devil has used deception to take their focus off God, as if there actually was a higher power. The devil is a lie. How can one truly recover by breaking the first commandment?

Could being politically correct be the cause of such a high rate of people relapsing after leaving drug and alcohol treatment centers? What higher power are they trusting in? God gives each of us free will to make decisions for ourselves. He is also a jealous God, and our decisions affect us and others. Although some of our decisions may affect others in different ways, accepting Christ as our savior (or not accepting Him) will only affect the outcome of our individual salvation.

Each of us must decide for ourselves to seek God and study His Word. He has given us a way to learn about His will for us, but it's up to us to educate ourselves. We cannot afford to just believe what other people tell us, for our souls are truly at stake. We must get into the habit of studying God's Word for ourselves so that we can develop a personal relationship with God, instead of just trying to live off the Christ in others.

The Christ in your pastor will not get you into heaven. It may be working out good for him, but you've got to get your own. The good news is that there's more than enough Christ to go around.

When it comes to accepting Christ, it's okay to be greedy; you can take all that you want. STUFF YOURSELF TODAY; it's good for you. Although the devil is constantly finding ways to remove Christ from our society, taking focus off God (by being more and more "politically correct"), the fact remains that there's no such thing as too much Jesus. The sad part is that not enough of us take the time to seek Him for ourselves.

I thank God for giving me a mind to seek Him. I also thank God for my deliverance from my addictions. I was using drugs and alcohol from the age of twelve to the age of forty-two. I've often wished that He would have delivered me from my addictions sooner, but if He had moved according to my will instead of His, what kind of insight would I have now? I give God praise for having perfect timing, and although I will never fully understand His will for my life, I will continue to trust in Him.

My Prayer

Heavenly Father, thank you for the provisions you've provided me with today. For the shelter and food that you've allowed me access to, Lord, thank you.

Father, today I pray that my faith be increased. Allow me to hear a word in a way that I can understand, and help me to explain it to others so that they too will understand.

Father, show through your word and my testimony that even though I'm unique I also share some of the same experiences that others have had. In doing so, Father, let your grace be shown. Today, let the light that is Christ be shown through me. Release the blessing of understanding and obedience to your Word so that I can receive your promise.

Father, remove the shields that the devil has set up to block those wanting to seek you but feel hopeless and unworthy due to something they heard, low self-esteem, addictions, lust of the flesh, and because of their worship of worldly possessions.

Father, give all who read this book and their families and friends the peace of mind and salvation that can only be found through Christ. Father, I also pray that I never get so comfortable with myself and my blessings that I take my focus off you.

In Jesus's name, I pray, praise, and claim to recover all that the devil took from me and more. Amen.

To everyone who reads this, remember that God is still in the blessing business, and my prayer is that He continues to do business with you. May God bless you as you are a blessing to others.

Now I would like to share with you part of my life journey in my worldly walk as I strayed from Christ and through grace I was forgiven. I would also like to share a few poems that I've written.

CHRIST INSURANCE

I am an anonymous sinner, and I USED TO BE AN ADDICT! Until God calls me home, I will be a SINNER IN RECOVERY! Believe me when I tell you God still performs miracles. I'm living proof because years ago (June 6, 2006, to be exact) I was living in a vacant house with a crack pipe in my hand having chest pains. Lucky for me, I had insurance that was paid in full. I'd prayed in the past that the Lord would help me get over my additions, but my prayers seemed to go on unanswered. My addiction started early at age twelve, just having a drink here and there.

I used to try to fit in by hanging with an older crowd doing "big-boy stuff." I mean, hey, what's wrong with drinking a little beer, smoking some weed, playing cards, and shooting dice with the fellas? Raised in church, I was told and believed that God sent His only Son to suffer and die for me and, that what Christ went through insured my chance for a better life. Insurance that would give me power to conquer anything that was against me.

I also believed that the devil never stops trying to keep you down, depressed, and with a broken spirit. Later in life, he had me lying to myself, saying that I could stop smoking crack if I'd really wanted to, but hey, I liked the high. I'm not hurting anyone, so I don't really have a problem. I'd work all week, cash my check, and, a few hours later, my forty-hour check was gone, along with my so-called friends.

I'd be alone feeling depressed again, and even worse, every once in a while, when I would see my daughter whom God has blessed me with, I'd see the shame in her eyes. She would have a look, like,

"That's my crackhead daddy, and I hope he doesn't see me or come over." It's rough when you get a look of "Oh, God, here he comes" from someone you love so much you'd die for them.

I give God praise, and I'm grateful for the miracle that happened on June 6, 2006, when I filed a claim for my Christ Insurance. Jesus died for me so that I may have a better life, and there's nothing He can't cure or do. I no longer suffer from the disease of addiction because of a miracle that has been paid for in full through my CHRIST INSURANCE.

I'm also here to let you know that whatever you may be going through if you're in need, the insurance that I have also covers you. All you have to do is file a claim by calling on Jesus.

My Father Told Me

My Father told me
To speak with you today
As for your situation
Help is on the way

My Father told me
No matter how dark the night
His Son is always with you
And Jesus is the light

My Father told me
Although you're down to your last dime
Not to let it concern you
Help will arrive on time

My Father told me
That He would provide all your needs
If you'd accept Christ as your shepherd
And follow where He leads

My Father told me
To sometimes just stand still
With my mouth closed and ears opened
To listen for His will

My Father told me
This message from above
THE DEVIL IS A LIE
AND OUR FATHER SENDS HIS LOVE

Written by Anonymous Sinner

Never

Never will I be under the influence again
To God I give thanks, in Jesus's name, amen
Never will I not encourage someone in need
Because of my deliverance, it's required of me
Never will I be perfect, trying to do God's will
But through my shortcomings, I know He loves me still
Never will I forget that Jesus paid the price
For my soul, my sins, my salvation, my life
Never again will I call myself an addict
For my Lord and Savior took away that bad habit
Never am I alone, of that I am faithful
So just for forever, I'll remain grateful
I'm a new creature, therefore I'm not the same
NEVER WILL A ROCK CRY OUT IN MY NAME!

Never will I forget that I used to be an addict and I give God praise
for my deliverance.

Written by Anonymous Sinner

LOOKING FOR A PLACE TO FIT IN

I was born the seventh child out of ten in March of 1964. I was also the only child out of ten whom my dad brought home from the hospital. Of course, I can't remember the trip, but at the beginning of my life, I like to think that he showed an interest in me—an interest that I would not be able to see from him later in life.

As far as I was concerned, my family was normal. Mom stayed at home, and Dad went to work. There were often times when my siblings and I had disagreements and sometimes fights, but although we sometimes fought each other, we'd always come together when someone outside the family started trouble. We were taught to walk, talk, and that if someone hit you, you were supposed to always hit back—unless it was an adult, of course. Adults where to be respected, always!

My dad always worked to make sure we had shelter and something to eat while my mother stayed at home and was the full-time babysitter, teacher, and nurse.

It was also my mother who took us to church and instilled in us as children God's love for us. If it had not been for my mother, I may have not known to call on Jesus in my times of need. Although I was lost and caught up in the way of the world, I still remembered that I was loved by God, that He loved me so much that He gave His Son as a sacrifice for me, and that according to my faith I would be forgiven and could do all things through Christ.

All I had to do was accept Christ as my savior and take the time to develop a personal relationship with God. Knowing about God's love for me was the only thing that gave me peace and a sense of hope during the mess that I was lost in. My mom taught me about what would later be my saving grace (the love of God).

As children in our household, we did not always have the latest styles in clothes or the most popular toys, but due to my dad's strong work ethic, none of us went to bed hungry. As a child, I did not realize the importance of a dad doing more than just going to work and bringing money into the household, that interacting with his child was very important. Later in life, I promised myself that I would be a better dad when I had children.

As an adult, I fell short of that goal with my daughter as well, due to addictions and growing up without an example of how a man should be with his child. My dad was an alcoholic, and although we lived under the same roof, I didn't really know him. I knew his name, he was my dad, he was married to Mom, he loved beer, and he kept a pistol in his pocket.

I don't know how his addiction got started, and I wish I'd had known him better. As a child, I felt as if I basically grew up in a single-parent home in which both parents lived. I'm grateful for my dad being there the best way he knew how, because many dads are completely absent.

Although he was around, I still felt resentment toward him because I grew up feeling I didn't really matter as much as I should have to him.

I often wondered what was so wrong with me that I wasn't even important to my own dad. What did I do? I know he loved me because he always went to work to provide for his family, although I can't remember him just coming out and telling me that he loved me. Except for whenever I got caught doing wrong, he often told me that he was going to beat me because he loved me and wanted me to learn to be a better person.

As I think back on some of those love displays, I remember thinking that I didn't really deserve so much love all at once, and I wish he'd stop being so affectionate. Spread the love with someone else for a while. Don't you love my sisters and brothers too? But as a child, I sometimes had to test my limits, and sometimes, when I got caught, Dad was just in a loving mood. Sometimes he just had one beer too many. A few times, even my neighbors showed love through beating me. What can I say, maybe I was loveable. In the end, it did teach me respect for others.

Still, I also wondered why I had to get into trouble to get attention. Was beer more important than I was? At the time, I didn't really understand, but my dad had an addiction. Later in life, I would understand addictions better as I developed one that was much worse and through Christ overcame it.

THERE WAS A VOID IN ME

As a child, I remember wanting and needing attention from my dad. Every once in a while, he'd give me a swallow of beer, and I remember feeling that at least for a while he noticed me.

However, as a child, I still needed more, but I realized Dad wasn't really the type to show emotions; after all, sometimes he did say hi when he came in from work, and I learned to accept that as enough. He'd then go off to watch TV or listen to some music while drinking a few beers.

I didn't understand exactly what all I needed, but I knew something was missing. There was a void in me that could only be filled by God, but at the time, I wasn't ready to except Christ in my life to the extent that I needed.

Even though my mother took me to church and taught me about our Father in heaven and I believed what I was taught, I still was not ready to surrender my life to Christ. I lived with my mom and dad, but it seemed like only Mom made time for me. Most dads on TV expressed an interest in their kids. Was that something that was made up just for entertainment or was it supposed to be that way?

It was a concept that I was unfamiliar with but I wish I had. What made my dad the way he was, I do not know. I'm sure he was a product of his environment as a child as well, but I have no idea what it was like for him growing up. What kind of dad was my grandfather? I wish I had a chance to know him after I went through rehab and stopped using, but unfortunately, he passed before God delivered me from my addictions. I'm sure our relationship would have been better now that I understand the addiction that I had and the nature of addictions, to some extent.

Growing up in a house of twelve, I had to fight for some attention, and since I couldn't get enough attention in the house, I went outside. Because I also was born premature, I was small for my age, and some kids my age who didn't know me thought I was too young for them to play with because kids my age were taller than I was.

To try to fit in, I had the brilliant idea to start hanging with older kids who knew me, thinking that somehow it would make me seem cooler and more mature. I would see some of them drinking and smoking cigarettes, and thought that was just what older people did. I thought that it wasn't no big deal.

Sometimes while hanging around the neighborhood, I would ask for something to drink and my "friends" would give me something. This was at age twelve. So just for some attention, confused and trying to find somewhere to fit in, I would hang around older kids, and I picked up bad habits. I now had somewhere I fitted in, and maybe I could even learn a few things here and there; after all, they were older than I was, so I was sure they knew more.

I remember from time to time some kids would go off to themselves to smoke in a garage. I'd sometimes stick my head in to see what was going on and noticed that the smoke didn't smell like normal cigarettes.

One day, I was pulled in and held down. While one of the older kids held me with my mouth covered, another blew what was called a shotgun in my face (a shotgun is where someone puts a joint in their mouths with the fire part in their mouths and blew smoke out the other end into another person's face), knowing that with my mouth covered sooner or later I would have to inhale and I would get high.

For the older kids, their addictions made seeing someone who was younger than them get high, funny to them. This happened to me several times and was how I was introduced to weed, and after getting high from being held down a few times, I later just asked for the joint to be passed to me.

So now I was drinking and smoking weed at age twelve. This would be something that I would do that went from just on occasions when I was around others that were getting high, to something I would do on a regular basis as I started to buy drugs for myself. It became a normal part of my life, and my addictions would continue to progress as I got older.

I started with a few sips of beer, to beer and weed, to wine and weed, to gin and weed, to weed and whatever was around to drink. In my mind, I saw nothing wrong with the way my life was. Surely I was not an addict because I never stole anything to get high. I didn't spend all my money on drugs, and I didn't always have to be high. I could stop whenever I wanted to. I just didn't want to because there wasn't anything wrong.

At age fifteen, getting high was certainly nothing new to me. I'd started skipping school to get high and be with girls who had issues with low self-esteem (completely unaware that I was trying to fit in because I had self-esteem issues of my own). I later dropped out of high school because I felt I wasn't learning anything on the one day a week I went to school, took a test, and passed it. I was now going to go to Job Corps to get my GED once I turned sixteen. I had plans to go into the army like one of my older brothers had done, once I had my GED and turned seventeen.

It seemed to be a plan, and since I wasn't an addict, all would be fine. I was going to be all I could be. And since I was more mature for my age due to all the time I spent hanging with older people, I would be able to handle the army. The addiction "that I didn't have" would prove me wrong. It would continue to grow and cause problems in my life as I lied to myself, denying that I had a problem. A problem I couldn't clearly see because most of the people I hung around had an addiction as well. So for me, it was kind of normal.

I couldn't understand why someone would want to be sober all the time. There was nothing wrong with being sober, but certainly there had to be some times when everyone wants to go to a party, and how can someone party without at least a drink? I was truly confused at how some people seemed to be happy being sober all the time.

THE LOSS OF MY BROTHER

At seventeen, a few months before I was to go to the army, my confusion would cause me to get into an argument with my older brother (the one who had been in the army). He had asked me to help clean the house, and instead of cleaning up, I started an argument with him because I had a joint in my pocket and wanted to go and get high. He could have just beaten me up until I changed my mind and helped with the cleaning, but instead, he chose to be a better person and just walked away.

He left the house, and about ten minutes later, I heard gunshots, and didn't really pay them no mind because gunshots where nothing new in my neighborhood. A couple of minutes later, there was a knock on the door and a person from the neighborhood saying that my brother had been shot.

Oh, this can't be right! I know I didn't hear what I thought I just heard—not my big brother! So me and my family ran down the alley to find my brother lying there bleeding out while waiting for an ambulance that would break down after it had arrived.

As I stood there watching my brother as the paramedics tried to help him, I was thinking how I wish I could apologize. I'm thinking, "I'm so sorry, please get up, big bro. Please move. I will do whatever you want me to do. Just show me a sign that you're still with me, please. Can you hear me, big bro? Can you at least move your hand? Please get up, please! I'm so sorry."

I don't know how long the family stood there before my brother was taken to the hospital, where they pronounced him dead. Oh, if ever I needed a drink, it's now. This is all my fault. If I hadn't started an argument, he would have stayed in the house. Why did I have to argue over something so stupid? I just wanted to go outside to smoke a joint. Dear God, let this be a dream and wake me up. Father in heaven, just wake me up and let me see my brother again.

Later, I got high until I passed out trying to get away from the pain, but I woke up the next morning and my big brother was still gone, the pain was still there, and my brother's death in my mind was still my fault, and it was unforgiveable. How will I live with and forgive myself for this? Maybe a stronger drink will help? Again I lied to myself.

Growing up, I was not taught to express my feelings. Talking about your feelings was something that rich people did with their private psychiatrist. There was no psychiatrist for the poor that I knew of, and getting emotional was also like showing a sign of weakness. So when things got a little rough, I dealt with it the only way I knew how: I held the pain in, and I turned to the doctor in the bottle.

The doctor in the bottle didn't judge me and always had time to listen. He also never helped, but at least he was always nearby. The devil saw to that, for he had seen into my future and tried to keep me from my destiny. He had me for a while, but the DEVIL IS A LIE. Though I still had to make it through years of addictions, I thank God for the grace He kept showing me.

ON MY OWN IN THE ARMY

In November 1981, I went off to the army. Now I was away from home a few months after my brother was murdered, after receiving no counseling, and I was giving a military ID at the age of seventeen. I was given an ID that allowed me to purchase alcohol for myself.

That was a reason to party. I no longer needed to get someone else to purchase alcohol for me. I can buy and drink whatever I wanted, when I wanted. I was now a military man. Wrong. I was a teenager with an addiction and who was in need of counseling, but instead, I got a license to drink while I was away from the support of my family.

So by day I went through the routine of military life while at night I sought after drugs, alcohol, and women to satisfy my addictions and my flesh while trying to bury the pain inside that I didn't know how to deal with. Even as I went through my daily routine on base, my thoughts would be about smoking some weed and looking for a bar to go to later. Maybe if I get high enough and spend some time with a girl I could get my mind off the loss of my brother. If only for a moment, I wouldn't have to see him lying there and I could block out what I had caused. Though I knew the devil did not have my best interest in mind and that he enjoyed my pain, at the time, I did not feel as if I deserved forgiveness.

I was lost, and the devil wanted to keep my mind clouded and my focus off God's love for me. At no time did the devil want me to remember that God's love was more than enough to help me through what I was going through. The more time I spent on me and the problems I had was less time spent on God. The one from which my help would come.

As my addictions progressed, so did my lust for the flesh. I was not interested in a serious relationship with a girl; all I wanted was someone to get high with and someone to have sex with. Therefore, there was no need for becoming friends or learning about any interest in what she may have had.

I was drawn to girls with low self-esteem and who felt as if getting high and having sex was a way for them to get and keep friends. Since I considered myself to be somehow damaged as well (since my dad had no interest in me), I sought others who were damaged as well. The devil knew my weaknesses, low self-esteem (my need to find somewhere to fit in and feel like I belonged), my addictions, and my lust of the flesh that was growing, and he used them against me every chance he had.

In 1982, I was sent to Korea, where my problems would escalate even more. There I was thrown into the world of prostitution. I had seen prostitutes in St. Louis, but not like this. In Korea, I could go into a bar and order a drink and a girl without even thinking about the police. Prostitutes and drinking seemed to be the military pastime.

Getting a girl was like ordering fast food, only faster. So I continued the routine of soldier boy by day and a drunken addict looking for sex by night. Even before I would ever hear of ED medications, we were buying pills that did the same thing, only they were ten pills for a dollar in Korea back in 1982. Soldiers would just use them for fun while having recreational sex with military women and Korean prostitutes. "It was just something to do" is the lie I kept telling myself (because I still didn't have a problem with any addiction).

My drinking and partying had gotten to the point where I would stay out all night instead of reporting back to base like I was supposed to. Most people knew me as Rodgers, but I had gotten the nickname Buck, maybe somehow as a reference to Buck Rodgers or maybe because I still hung around with people older than I was. That made me the young buck in the group. The friend who gave me the nickname also made up a slogan for me that didn't help my attitude. They called me Buck because I didn't give a f—.

I was a teenager who needed counseling, with an attitude, and had a problem with alcohol. Even though I was ordered to seek treatment for alcoholism, put on restriction, and fined, that did not stop me; after all, I didn't have an alcohol problem anyway. I just wanted a drink.

While on restriction, since I couldn't get out the front gate, I took some bolt cutters to cut a hole in the fence out of the guards' sight so that I could come and go as I pleased.

One day, a fellow soldier had given me a small razor that I would later sneak off base with (the devil was setting me up). Later that night, I was getting drunk with a friend, and I don't know what led up to it, but he had started beating up a prostitute. A Korean cabdriver had seen what my friend was doing and attempted to sneak up behind him and was about to stab him in the back with a screwdriver.

Before he could reach my friend, I came up behind him and sliced his back up with the razor I'd been given earlier. I thank God it was cold outside and the cabdriver had on a jacket, which minimized the damage I could have caused.

This was in February of 1983, on a night when I was supposed to be restricted to base. Things where looking bad for me. If the devil would have had his way, I would have been in a Korean prison by age nineteen, but God saw that the devil was going too far, and He showed me grace. If the Korean cabdriver had pressed charges, I would have been in big trouble.

However, I had another friend who knew the cabdriver and knew that the driver also sold drugs. So my friend told the cabdriver that if he pressed charges against me that the authorities would find out about his drug dealings. So the charges against me were dropped because the driver didn't press charges. God is good!

Due to the trouble I'd been in and my addiction to alcohol, I was discharged for failing alcohol rehabilitation instead of locked up for assault. Through all my mess, God was still with me, but I still had issues to deal with. I just had to realize I couldn't deal with them alone. This would take more years of me lying to myself, telling myself that I was in control and that I didn't have a problem because I was not an alcoholic or an addict.

ADDICTIONS AFTER THE ARMY

So I left the army with an extra addiction (sex), and I was now drinking more. Although I was welcomed back home with open arms, my addiction problem still went unaddressed. There's a saying, and I can't remember exactly how it goes, but it's something like "There's an elephant in the room, but no one wants to acknowledge it," as if everything will be okay as long as we don't talk about it. If you ignore it, then it will go away.

Then there was the "man attitude," where real men don't cry about their situations and they don't need help getting out of them. If a real man got into something, then he can get out of it on his own.

Asking for help was kind of like showing a sign of weakness or begging, and a man should be able to do for himself. If he got himself into a situation, he should be able to get himself out of it on his own. Like I said, I was confused; I just didn't realize how much. Anyway, now that I'm back home, it's a good time to catch up with old friends and for a party. I can't walk into a bar and buy liquor anymore, but I can get someone else to buy me something before I go to a club, and I can buy weed myself.

Now I was back home, but I was still doing what I was doing in the army, getting high and looking for girls, as if that was all I needed in life. It didn't matter if the girl was supposed to have a boyfriend or not; all that mattered was will she come with me and how much she will let me get away with. If she was not high, I would try to get her high; if she was high, I would try to get her higher. The higher she was, the easier it was for me to get what I wanted, and the higher I was, the lower my standards where.

Sometimes the girls did not even have to be high, but I had to be. Depending on how much I had to drink, some girls changed from an ugly thing to a beauty queen, and at the time, I had to get with them. After my high came down, then I had to get away. But while I was high, nothing else mattered.

The fact that the girl was someone's mother, daughter, or sister and deserved to be respected as one of God's creations did not matter to me; I just had to satisfy my flesh. I also never even thought of or heard of sex as an addiction; therefore, this was something else that I had no problem with. I was just a normal teenager (confused) without a clue as to how much I thought I knew but didn't know. In the words that my dad would use, "I was an educated dummy."

After a few months of celebrating my return home, I still felt a void each time my high came down. What is it? I'm missing something, and I can't quite put a finger on it. Could it be that I stopped going to church on a regular basis at age twelve? No, that can't be it, because my mom taught me about God and I know that He still loves me. As long as I believe in God, I don't have to go to church on a regular basis, do I? Those "church people" are no better than I am, anyway. I don't need to be all "godly" right now; I just need something to do before and after I get high. God will always be there.

I know what I can do: I can go back to Job Corps and learn something, get an allowance, and I can stay on campus this time. I needed something to fill some of my time. I know there has to be more to life than this. The more I focused on me, myself, and I, the less I focused on God, and the more I would become lost. I didn't consider the fact that God said in His Word that He was a jealous God and that nothing should come before Him. Yet I chose to put myself and my addictions first.

I was in desperate need of a different mind-set, but I was confused and didn't realize it. So I continued on in the world of "Only I mattered," and the more I thought that I was in control, the more control I gave away to the ways of the world. I smoked and sold weed on campus, and I would also sneak alcohol on campus to sell as well. Everything seemed cool for a while. I always had money in my pocket, and although I was never really the social type, I seemed to have a few friends. Unfortunately, I can't remember most of their names. Some of them may have been blessings I missed because at the time they didn't matter to me. Everything was about me.

I remember two people from my time at Job Corps: a girl named Helen, because she was a friend and because she was what we called "thick," and a friend named Steve because we were partners in crime. Steve and I had a few things in common: we both liked money and girls, and thought that most things that were important were about us. We sold our products together, and when one of us was off campus, the other was still there making sells.

What we were doing wasn't right, but we had each other's back. We were friends, and I had no clue that my friend Steve would later be a blessing in my life. (You never know who, what, when, or where God will use a situation to bless you with.)

Even though the devil was trying to set me up, I thank God because so was He. Only difference is that God was setting me up for a future blessing. After Job Corps, I continued to sell weed, mainly just so that I could make money to support my drinking and so that I'd always have something to smoke myself. I'd work at jobs that had nothing to do with what I had trained for in Job Corps, but just so that I could afford a place to stay without taking a drug test to get the job.

Although I had a few dollars in my pocket, somewhere to stay, I was able to support my habits (not addictions, because I was not an addict), and though from time to time I had the company of a girl, something was still missing.

MY GIRL, MY BABY GIRL

Maybe it was time for a girlfriend, someone whose name I could remember and that would actually mean something to me. This would be a big step. Now I would have to work on considering someone's feelings other than mine. If others can do it, then so can I.

So I took a chance and started a relationship. The relationship didn't start off right because although I was trying something new, I still hadn't changed my mind-set. My mind-set was set on outside of family and work a girl was only good for sex. If I had to wait more than a week or two to get some, then I was wasting my time; a girl that was just a friend was useless.

So I met a girl, and we had sex before we had really gotten to know each other, just like every other girl I'd been with.

We moved in together, and things seemed to be okay. We both liked to smoke weed, drink, and have sex. I was kind of content in thinking that it was no longer all about me but now it was about us (when it should have been about God first). I now had someone to share things with on a different level, and it was cool. Here I was at age twenty-two, in my first serious relationship, which started after we had already had sex.

This was part of the same story of my life: I would take time to get to know something about a girl after sex basically so that I could have more sex with her. That was the mind-set I had. I would just listen to her long enough to get what I wanted and tell her whatever I thought she wanted to hear (something my older brother had told me he heard from my brother who was murdered).

However, there was something a little different about this girl. Yes, she had a nice smile and a nice body, but she also had a way of actually making me want to hear what she had to talk about sometimes. For me, that was unusual, but I enjoyed it. Somehow, I cared about someone else. Could this be that love thing I've heard about? If this is then this is nice. Unfortunately, it would not last.

Later in our relationship, on June 28, 1988, we had our daughter. I had a baby girl and loved her at second sight (she looked much better after the nurses cleaned her up.) Later, I can remember lying in bed playing with her when she was about nine months old. I was in bed, and her mother had laid her on my chest, and I had covered my face with the cover, playing like I was hiding. My daughter pulled the cover off my face and smiled at me.

To this date, that was the most beautiful thing I've ever seen. Without consideration, she was now the most important thing in my life. I loved her more than myself and had to do all I could for her, and I still didn't think about going to church or attempting to find out what God's will was.

I was now a daddy, and I was going to be better than my dad was, yet I never thought about making God the head of my family. I was still confused and missing something in my life. I remembered my mother teaching me about God's Word; I just did not apply it in my life.

God was the missing part of my life, but I wasn't ready to include Him because that would've taken time away from me and what I wanted. I'm so grateful that God is not a man, for if He was, He would have surely given up on me. Instead, God just gave me more time because He knew that one day I would get sick and tired of being sick and tired, and call on the savior my mom told me about.

Before my daughter's first birthday, me and her mother had broken up. I had been betrayed by the girl I loved. Or did I also betray myself and her by not putting God first in our relationship? All of a sudden, the emptiness inside of me had grown. I was now experiencing a different type of pain.

MY INTRODUCTION TO CRACK

I now had one more thing that I didn't quite know how to deal with. Since I knew of no one I could talk to about it, I tried something that I was familiar with. I got high as I started to seek out women with low self-esteem and who wanted to get high also.

To try to drown out this new pain, I started revisiting the old neighborhood hangout more often. It was the familiar place where I'd gone to get high for years; it was also the place where I'd watched my older brother lie bleeding out on the street moments after we had an argument. It was where for the first time I would hear someone take their last breath.

I was always welcome there because I had a history with the people there and I wasn't the type to always come broke or begging. I always had something or had some money on something. Since I started revisiting the hangout more, I noticed that something was different. Most of the time, everyone used to stay on the first floor and play cards, shoot dice, drink, and smoke weed. Now all of a sudden, certain people kept going upstairs for some reason. Me, being curious and not wanting to be left out (still trying to fit in), I went upstairs and stuck my head in yet another door, and I was invited in.

They were smoking something on a glass pipe, and it wasn't weed. This was something new to me. Since I was supposed to be "cool" and had some money, my "friends" offered me some of what they were smoking for free and showed me how to smoke it. I had now had my introduction to crack, the drug where the first hit was free, but for the years to come, it would cost me more than I could've ever imagined.

In the years to come, I would spend money in the pursuit of the feeling that I got from the first hit. A feeling that I would never get no matter how much I spent. I kept in contact with my daughter's mother and even tried to work things out for a while, but I was unwilling and didn't know how to completely forgive. My addiction was getting worse also.

Later, my daughter's mother moved to Baltimore, Maryland, where I pretty much lost track of her and my daughter. Every once in a while, I would hear from my daughter's aunt, and they would tell me that they would speak to their sister off and on whenever they could find her. I often wondered, where was my baby girl? Was she okay, and how could I have failed her like this?

I was officially worse than my dad because he at least knew where I was. As if not knowing where my daughter was most of the time wasn't enough, I later discovered her mother had developed a worse addiction also. Despite our disagreements, she was still my friend and the mother of my daughter. I would not even wish an addiction on an enemy, and I wish I could have helped my friend, but I was unable to help even myself at the time.

My friend was and still is in my prayers. May God bless and keep her.

Now, I've been around mothers with addictions, and most I've seen weren't the best role models even though they loved their children and their children loved them. It's not because they felt as if their kids were not deserving of better parenting, but it's because of a lack of knowledge of how to deal with and overcome an addiction. An addiction that was the result of a bad decision or an experience they had that in some way may have left them confused and feeling as if they had no one to turn to.

This, in my opinion, is true for both moms and dads dealing with addictions. So where could someone find knowledge of how to deal with an addiction? Most addicts can't afford to check into exclusive treatment centers for help and to receive some knowledge of how to deal with their addiction. (Most people aren't helped at exclusive centers either.) They are also often told that they would always be an addict anyway, so without knowledge of what God said, they hear and believe what man tells them.

This causes some addicts to just accept defeat, and they give in to their addiction. I praise God for giving me the mind to not just accept defeat. For I knew that through Christ I was capable of doing anything, that by His stripes I am healed, and that I am more than a conqueror.

My problem was that I needed to learn how to change my mind-set. I also had to learn how to tap into the God Love that my mother taught me about. It was always there, and I knew that God had the power to change things and that all things where possible through Christ, but I had no real knowledge of how to use my faith.

I basically would pray and then cancel out some of my prayers by praying for some things with doubts. It would be years later when I would understand that doubts were the opposite of faith and that God would move where there was faith. I was not sure of the best way to pray, but I knew that prayer was important. So I continued to pray the best way that I knew how. I prayed for a better understanding of God's Word and that one day God would help me out of my situation.

SEEMED LIKE I'D FALLEN
AND COULDN'T GET UP

As the years went by, I would go in between from being a functional addict (able to go to work and keep a place of my own to stay) to being homeless going to work and spending most of my check getting high and sleeping wherever I could. Sometimes I would stay with family members for a while, and sometimes, I slept on park benches, in vacant buildings, or at bus stops.

How did I get here? I'd seen alcoholics, addicts, and homeless people growing up, but I never imagined that I would become one of them. Now I was all three. It seemed like I'd fallen and couldn't get up.

At first, getting high was just a way to fit in and party; now it was getting in the way of my life. It had now become who I was. Before I started getting high, I used to tell my mother that I wanted to be a chef when I grew up. Before age twelve, I had dreams for my future, but all those dreams were lost as I tried to find somewhere to fit in. Somehow, trying to find a place to fit in only alienated me more as I often tried to hide being high.

As I would go around others who weren't high, I would be paranoid, wondering if they could smell the alcohol on my breath or the weed in my clothes. I wondered if the Visine had cleared my eyes up. Was my facial expression different, or were my eyes too wide open after hitting the crack pipe? Would people see me coming and think, "Here comes the crackhead" or "How can someone so smart be so dumb and choose to smoke and drink their lives away at such a young age?"

To be an addict was never a career choice of mine as a child, but it was what I'd become. Being an alcoholic now had even given me something in common with my dad, but still, there was an emptiness inside me that couldn't be filled no matter how much drugs and alcohol I put into it. I was so focused on trying to understand why I couldn't get the love I thought I should get from my dad that I lost focus of the love of my Father in heaven.

Instead of placing God first in my life at all times, He had become one of the bottom 5 in my life. Most of the time, God came in fourth or fifth place. From time to time, He would become number 1 in my life for a brief moment, depending on the situation I was in.

My mother had taught me better than that. She taught me that God was above all things and that my life would be better if I would learn to put Him first, but being the educated dummy that I was, I decided that I knew what was best for me. Once again I'd lied to myself.

I thank God for all those who kept me in their prayers. I believe that because of the faith of others that God sent angels to watch over me until my faith had developed more. I also know that the faith of others can only get me so far and that I must take the time to develop a personal relationship with God so that my faith will continue to grow.

No one can get to heaven on the faith of others. We can only get to the Father through Christ, and because of the price Christ paid on Calvary, each of us now have access to the Father, but it is our faith that pleases God and causes Him to show up.

In the back of my mind, I knew all this because of what I was taught as a child. My problem was that as I grew older I used my free will to put more things of the world ahead of God's will, and that only caused more problems. For years I went from place to place, working where I could and blowing all my money getting high, as if only the dope man's bills mattered. I was unaware that when I started getting high at the age of twelve that part of my mind-set would also stay at age twelve.

So instead of acting my age, I depended on others to give me a place to stay. The money I made was just for me and what I wanted. Most of the time, paying bills like a grownup was not what I wanted. I'm not saying that all homeless people are childish, because everyone's situations are different and every homeless person does not have an addiction, but this was how it was for me, and I believe the same is true for a lot of addicts, whether they admit it or not.

THE PASSING OF MY DAD

It was maybe the end of 1995 or the beginning of 1996 that I had a dream that something was wrong with my dad. I can't remember the details, but I know that when I woke up I felt as if something was wrong.

I was staying with a brother-in-law at the time, and I left to go visit my parents. When I arrived, I found out that my dad had been diagnosed with cancer and that they had caught it too late. The doctors said that he would only have about three months to live. He had been sick for a while, but due to his high tolerance for pain and all his self-medicating, no one knew how sick he was until the pain had gotten to be unbearable and he went to the hospital.

Later, they operated on him, sent him home, and tried to make him as comfortable as possible during his last few months that they said he had. God had given my family something that's not given to most: a chance to say goodbye to a loved one.

Though the doctors said my dad had about three months to live, my dad lived over another year. I wish that I had been more mature at the time; maybe I would have thought of more meaningful conversations to have with my dad during his last days. At least I could have prayed with him.

I know that he knew of God because you couldn't be around my mother that long without hearing about God, but I don't know how his personal relationship with God was. Knowing that his time was coming to an end, did he accept Christ as his savior? I have no idea. At the time, my mind-set of a twelve-year-old pretty much only allowed me to watch TV with him while having a beer.

For us, we loved each other the best way we knew how, and I thank God for the time I had to just sit with my dad. However, I still wonder what made him the way he was. What sparked his addiction to alcohol? How long has the curse of addiction been on my family? I don't know, but I give God praise and thanks for breaking the curse of addictions from me. I also pray that I may be used to help someone else.

On March 26, 1997, my dad passed away early that morning, maybe around 2:00 or 3:00 a.m. I was staying down the street from my parents in my cousin's basement, sleeping on a couch. At that time, I was awakened by the news of my dad's passing and was told to go find another family member who was also dealing with addictions. Since we were the addicts in the family, we knew where to find each other because we hung out in some of the same circles.

So I walked about a mile away to the vacant apartment building that they were living in to the fourth floor, where they were staying in a vacant apartment, woke them up, and told them the news.

Together we walked back to my parents' to meet up with the rest of the family and then waited for my dad's body to be picked up. Our dad was no longer with us. He was never the type to express his love with words, but he expressed it the best way he knew how. He expressed it by going to work to make sure that all ten of his kids never went to bed hungry or homeless. After we were grown, then we were on our own.

I HAD ANGELS WATCHING OVER ME

Uncertain of how to deal with the passing of my dad, I did what I was familiar with: I got high, as if that was the answer for all things. If I was confused, I got high. If I was hurting, I got high. If I was happy, I got high. Whenever I had mixed emotions that I didn't know how to deal with, I got high.

I loved my dad, but I also felt resentment toward him because I felt as if I just wasn't important enough to him. He always seemed to have more time for beer than he had for me. Not realizing that this was not the man but the addiction.

It was a family curse that was affecting me also, even though I was in denial of the fact. After all, I didn't really have a problem; I just liked to get high. So there I was, I had witnessed a brother take his last breath after we had an argument, I don't know where my daughter is or if she's okay, and my dad had passed away, and I'm not sure how to feel about that.

What to do? What to do? In my confusion, I might as well turn to the doctor in a bottle. It's true that he never helps the problems, but at least for a while I can forget about them, and in some cases, I'd even get a second opinion from Dr. Crack, and his diagnosis was always "Just have another hit."

Now I'm really messed up as I keep hearing the doctors tell me that all I need is just one more hit and it will all be okay. I've lied to myself so much that now I'm starting to believe my addictions. So I did what I could to get another hit. I thank God for hearing all the prayers that were made on my behalf. I know that angels were watching over me because throughout my years of getting high I've been robbed at gunpoint several times. Even though there have been cases here in St. Louis where a person was robbed and the robber shot them even after they took their money, I was not one of those cases.

I've had a gun put to my head twice, once going into a dark alley trying to buy drugs and once going into a dark gangway. One time, a guy even pretended like he had drugs and snatched the money out of my hand and ran. Like an idiot, thinking of the drug money instead of my safety, I chased him into a yard where his people where. I wasn't paying attention to where I was going until the guy on the porch pulled out a 38 pistol and asked me what was up. I told him that the other guy had run off with my money and I was trying to get it back.

For some reason, he respected my crackheadedness and told the dude to give me back my money, then he proceeded to tell me to get my blank-blank away from his house. At this time, the movie *The Matrix* had not came out yet, and I couldn't imagine dodging bullets, so I took my money and walked my blank-blank down the street. Normally on the streets, I would not appreciate being called blank-blank, but if I ever had to accept being called one, this seemed to be a good time. So I thanked the gentleman for being so polite, and I moved on.

Another time angels were watching over me while I was in my mess, I was hit by a car. I was staying in an apartment with my girl-friend, and we had company over and we were getting high. After the drugs ran out, I was on my way to get some more crack and something more to drink. As I left the apartment, I stood at the light, and when it turned green, I noticed a car across the street to my left, and it didn't have its turn signal on, so I proceeded to cross the street.

As I got to the center of the street, the car came speeding around the corner as if this was a video game and he was trying to get some bonus points by running me down. I had nowhere to go, and something told me to just jump, so I did.

That jump saved my life. It was kind of like what you're told to do if you're on fire. Stop, drop, and roll. I stopped when I smashed into the windshield, then as the car speeded off as if he couldn't see or hear 180 pounds going into the windshield, I went up over the car and dropped to the ground, and then I rolled.

I thank God another car wasn't behind the one that hit me and for the whisper of an angel in my ear that told me to jump, otherwise I would have been under the car as it kept going. When my roll came to a stop, I got up, dusted myself off, and I noticed that nothing was broken, so I went on to buy some crack.

When I got back home, my girlfriend noticed that I didn't have anything to drink and that I was dirty, so she asked me what had happened, and I told her that I had been hit by a car on my way to get the crack.

Her response was "You got hit by a car and then you got up and went to get some crack?" I told her yes, and she asked me if I was okay. At that time, she was laughing at me, but she asked if I was okay.

My response was something like, "Ha-ha-ha, give me that pipe. I just got hit. Now I need a hit" (PS: that's not funny, I had a problem, so stop laughing). The next morning, I felt the pain, and I walked with a limp for a while.

I WAS STARTING TO GET
TIRED OF GETTING HIGH

My addictions continued for yet a few more years, and by now, crack had become number 1 on my most wanted list. Crack was now what I went to work for. Paying bills didn't matter. I would go to work waiting for payday, and sometimes during the week, I would imagine buying something other than drugs and alcohol. Sometimes I would even make plans to do something different, but eventually, I would end up smoking and drinking my check away.

Through all this, I somehow convinced myself that my problem wasn't that bad. At least I was supporting my own habit and wasn't stealing or robbing anyone so I was okay. I was a crackhead whom you could trust in your home.

Some nights I was not sure where I was going to sleep, and sometimes, my feet were almost coming through the soles of my shoes, but it was all good. At the end of a forty-hour week, I could party for a few hours and all my "friends" would remember where to find me. I was the man until the crack was gone, and then I was just me. It was okay that everyone had an emergency and had to leave at the same time after the crack was gone every week. That's no problem because next week will be different. The following week, I would lie to myself again.

Crack had my mind messed up. I didn't want to be around people whom I knew would always leave when my money was gone, yet most of the time I didn't want to get high alone. I knew that no matter how much crack I smoked that nothing would have the same effect as the first hit of the day, yet I continued to spend my money trying to get that feeling I had from the first hit. I'd end up spending hundreds a week chasing a feeling even after I had promised myself that this check I was only going to buy just one rock. Well, "Oops, I lied again."

How could I have done this again? I spent all my money getting high, and I have nothing to show for it except a burnt-out cigarette lighter and crack pipe. It's okay, next week will be different. LORD, PLEASE HELP ME!

I know it was the prayers of others that kept me out of more serious trouble, and after a while, I started saying short prayers for myself. I'm not sure when it started, but after a while, getting high was no longer fun or cool. I was starting to see it as a problem but didn't know what to do about it. Sometimes all I could say was, "Lord, help me."

There were times when I wasn't sure what I was supposed to be doing or even who I was, but I knew there was more to life than just getting high. Just getting high wasn't helping me. The problems I had seemed to not be so bad when I was high, but every time my high came down, my problems were still there.

I also knew that just another neighborhood crackhead was not who I wanted to be. I was better than that. Was there hope for me? I believed all things were possible through Christ, but maybe I shouldn't have stopped going to church and maybe I'd missed something. LORD, HELP ME!

I know now that at the time the Lord was already working on my breakthrough because I was starting to get tired of getting high. I just wasn't tired enough.

LORD, HELP ME TO DO SOMETHING RIGHT

While I was still working to support several of the neighborhood liquor stores and crack dealers, in 2000, I received a message that my daughter had recently witnessed her mother being shot and that the state was about to take her and her brother if no one sent for them.

I desperately wanted to get in contact with my daughter, but not like this. I thank God the man didn't hurt the kids and that her mom survived, but I can't imagine how much of an impact that incident has had on her life. I'm grateful and proud of the way she has grown up.

To this date, we still haven't talked about that incident, but she and her brother seem to be okay and are doing a great job raising their own families. Today I am grateful that God watched over them. Back then, my only prayer was that God give me the wisdom and strength to do something right with my check that week.

My prayer was, "Lord, please give me the mind-set to purchase the plane tickets before I purchase some crack and something to drink." This was my prayer that day because every week I'd lie to myself, saying that I wasn't going to get high or I wasn't going to spend all my money on getting high. Despite all my intentions of taking a crack break, I'd end up blowing all my money once again—all in the name of trying to create the feeling of my first hit of the day.

Father, please help me get my baby girl and her brother back to St. Louis. At this moment, Father, things are crucial, and I know that without you, Lord, I'd only mess things up. I've come to the realization that I do not always make the best decisions, and this decision is much too important for me to handle on my own.

Father, stay with me as I cash my check and guide my footsteps toward the ticket counter instead of the liquor counter and crack dealer. Lord, help me do something right.

I give God praise and thanks for allowing me to be around family and friends who helped me get to the airport and to get tickets even while the thought of "I could go get the tickets after I got just one hit" lingered in the back of my mind. The devil is a lie!

I thank God for allowing me to remember something my dad used to tell all his kids, and that was for us to "stop and think." After giving "Just one hit" some thought, I knew that if I'd gone for one and tried to get to the airport later I wouldn't have made it. If it had not been for God and His grace, I surely would have messed up the chance to see my daughter again, and for that, forever is not enough time to give Him thanks.

I also give thanks because He still continues to show me grace even though I continue to make mistakes. God is good!

MAYBE I DO HAVE A PROBLEM

Praise God for getting my daughter and her brother back to St. Louis safely! Things are about to be different now. I'm so glad I don't have a serious problem with getting high and I can stop whenever I want to. All I have to do is put my mind to it and I can do it.

Last week, my check was used, along with the help of family, to buy plane tickets, and now that my baby girl's here, it's time to celebrate. I'll get me a case of beer, maybe a pint of some hard liquor, and just one crack rock. That will be all I need to have a nice weekend, and maybe I can do something for my daughter and her brother also. I know that they need me and I have to step up, but after working all week, I deserve some time to relax and enjoy myself. So all I'll do is get high for a while, and then I will go and take care of home.

Once again, things would not go as planned. Somehow once again buying just one $20 rock turned into me being in an alley or vacant building trying to get the last hit off a crack pipe, several hundreds of dollars later. It was never my intention to smoke up all my money again and stay out so long, but now that I'm broke and it's too late to go to my sister's house after she's taken me and the kids in, I'll just sleep for a couple of hours outside again. Later, I'll go home, apologize to my sister, and next week I'll do better.

I've got to because the kids need me, and since my sister's letting us stay at her house, the least I could do is contribute to the house. This is the last time I will go out like this. All my so-called friends always have to go after the dope is gone anyway, and I could spend less money getting high alone. That's what I'll start doing. I'll be saving money, and my crack will last longer if I'm smoking alone.

Somehow at the time, that twisted way of thinking made sense to me, and since I'd already messed up and knew that I messed up badly, it was a way for me to lie to myself as if things weren't as bad as they seemed. I was still not ready to admit that things were as bad as they were, but I was starting to realize that I did need to make changes in my life. No longer was it just me, my crack, and I; now my baby girl and her brother were here, and they needed help.

I wanted to help them, but I didn't know how. What words could I use to get through to them while I was high? How can I talk to them about what they'd seen and been through while I was high? Will it be possible for me to help them even though I can't help myself, while I'm high?

Lord, help me. Father, I'm lost and in need of your help. Please help me to make better decisions for myself and the kids. In Jesus's name, I pray, amen.

Well, I guess for now all I can do is try to be around. I'm not sure what to do, but I will keep telling my daughter that I love her and try to give her a hug even though she always pushes me away. It is as if she hates me and I bother her by breathing. I don't know what her mother told her about me, and I'm not about to talk bad about her mother to her. All I know is that she goes out of her way to ignore me, and that's disrespectful. I love her more than I can say, yet all she shows is hatred toward me.

While staying with one of my sisters, she'd come in from school. After I opened the door and said hello to her, she would walk past me to go say hello to my sister, my sister's kids, and then go to say hi to the dog in the basement. As I'm watching this, I'm thinking to myself, "Lord, please help me deal with this girl," because I know I'd be wrong for helping her down the basement steps to say hello to the dog by punching her in the back of her head.

But no, I can't do that. I'm not about to hurt my baby girl, and I better not catch anyone else trying to hurt her. I just wish that I could get through to her, but she won't even talk to me. Her attitude bothers me, but I understand she's been through a bad experience, and I'm not sure how to help her deal with it. I also realize that part of her attitude is because of her bloodline, so I'll just leave and go have myself a few drinks.

At least on the streets I don't have to put up with people being disrespectful to me because I don't care about them, don't have to be around them, and I could walk away or hit them in the head with something without feeling bad later. At least as long as I had a drink or some dope I could find someone who understood me and didn't mind me hanging around.

Although what I wanted the most was just to hold my baby girl. I had not seen her most of her life, nor did I even know where she was or how she was doing.

I understand if she felt that I had let her down by not being around, and I couldn't blame her for that. Was everything she had gone through partly my fault? Do I really mess up everything? Maybe I do have a problem. God allowed me to see her again, and I'm blowing money getting high while she and her brother need help.

Lord, help me figure out what to do. I know that I am more than a conqueror. I AM MORE THAN A CONQUEROR! But how can I conquer these addictions?

I will figure it out because I am a MAN. I was a M-A-N, all right. I was a M-misguided, A-addicted, N-numbskull! I thought since I had gotten myself where I was on my own then I could overcome my situation on my own.

So I decided that I would just stop smoking crack but continue to drink pretty much anything around and every once in a while smoke some weed. I could handle that; after all, I am a MAN.

That was the plan, but I was smoking crack for so long that smoking for a little while longer wouldn't hurt. So I will give crack up later, maybe next week or the week after that.

The kids and I stayed at a few different places for a while, and eventually, they moved in with their aunt. I continued to bounce around from place to place, sometimes in rooming houses and sometimes in vacant buildings. Somewhere along the line of me giving up crack (each time I ran out of crack and was broke again), I started having chest pains whenever I would smoke crack.

I'd personally known people who have died from heart attacks while getting high trying to smoke too much at once. I knew people who were beaten up, robbed, and killed in vacant buildings. Even though I knew some of the risks involved with my lifestyle, this was my life at the time. Though it was like the wild kingdom where the weak are taken out, I had learned how to deal with situations as they arrived, and showing weakness was not an option.

Sometimes while getting high in vacant buildings I would start having chest pains and stop and pray that I would not die alone in a vacant building with a crack pipe in my hand. Sometimes if I was alone having chest pains I'd go find someone to get high with, or if I was around other people in a vacant building and didn't know them well, when I started having chest pains, I'd have one hand on my chest and one hand on my knife, thinking to myself that there has to be more to life than this.

Other times, the devil would say, "Roll up a primo [crack smashed up and rolled up in tobacco or weed]. Don't use the crack pipe right now." Because my chest didn't hurt as much when I smoked primos. My mind was not on throwing the crack away because I was having chest pains.

The devil was telling me, "This is some good crack, and you don't even have to smoke a lot all at once. Stretch it out, take smaller hits, and it will last longer. Your heart is already slowing down. You're okay. Have another hit. THAT'S SOME GOOD CRACK, YUUUUMMMM!"

There were times I would attempt to stop smoking crack on my own, and after a while, if I went more than a few days without getting high, the devil would have someone with some crack to remember where to find me. Most of the time, when I wanted to get high, people with money did not remember me. Now all of a sudden, since I'm trying to stop smoking crack, here comes a "friend" with some. (The devil will always show up more aggressively when he knows you're starting to take some of your focus off the world to put it on God.)

There were times when I tried just drinking for a while, but whenever I had more than a few dollars in my pocket for a few days, my couple of drinks turned into a drink and a rock, plus one more, and another, to I may as well spend the rest of what I have. Once again, I would find myself displeased with the outcome of my day, because I had messed up yet again trying to overcome my addiction to crack on my own.

Later, I found out that part of my problem with addictions was my mind-set (the way I was thinking). My mind-set was telling me that crack was my only problem. I was not willing to admit that my drinking always led me to smoking. Oftentimes, I would get discouraged after I tried and failed, tried and failed, and tried and failed again.

The devil wants people to remain discouraged because it's easier to keep someone down when they feel hopeless. I knew people who have gone to rehab and came out looking better, sometimes for months, but after hanging around the familiar places for a while, they start doing the old familiar things (getting high). Seeing that didn't give me much hope for my situation.

However, there was an old friend from Job Corps (Steve) whom God allowed me to come across from time to time over a period of several years. This was not just someone whom I had heard about who had stopped getting high and was doing better. This was a friend whom I had gotten high with and he was clean for years. Running into him from time to time was an unexpected blessing. I didn't tell him this because at the time, I did not realize how important it was for me to see a friend from time to time who was no longer using.

I had always had the attitude that if one man could learn how to do something then so could I. Seeing my friend from time to time gave me hope for my situation, and I needed hope. I'm also grateful for all the prayers of my family and friends on my behalf. I completely understand that if it had not been for the prayers of others and the grace of God that I may have died alone in a vacant building. But God showed me favor.

I COULDN'T FIGHT MY
DEMONS ALONE

I can remember one day I was leaving a twenty-four-hour check-cashing place on my way to the dope set when a lady stopped me. She said that she saw that God had some kind of purpose for me, and she asked if she could pray for me. She did not say what the purpose was; she just said that she saw something in me.

Although my main goal at the time was to get to the dope set, I was smart enough to accept prayer. So she prayed for me, and I thanked her and thanked God for her prayers and allowing me to see another day. I also asked Him to watch over me even though I knew what I was about to do was wrong. I'm so glad to have a God who shows love even when we're wrong.

Around the same time, I also started having a recurring dream. I can't remember exactly when it started, but maybe it was around the years 1998–99. I know that it stopped around the end of 2008. I would have this dream once or twice a year, and it would always be the same. It would be like I was dreaming that I was dreaming.

In my dream, I would be lying in bed asleep, and when I opened my eyes, I was surrounded by three demons. All I could see was three dark shadows, and I knew they were demons because I felt as if I was surrounded by evil.

So I tried to get up, and one would grab my mouth, one grabbed my hands, and the other grabbed my feet. Then it seemed as if they wanted to take me somewhere, and I wasn't real crazy about that idea, so I started to try to fight.

In the dream, in my mind, I knew it was a dream and that I would be okay if I could just wake up. I also felt as if I was in a fight that I knew that I could not win alone, and I needed help. I was fighting for my soul. If I could only call on the name that my mom told me about, I would be okay. So I tried to call on the name above all names, but as one of the demons was covering my mouth all I could get out was "Je."

I knew that I was in trouble now. Things were not looking good, but I had to keep fighting to call on the name from where my help would come, but still, all I could get out was "Je." Now the situation was getting too serious. "Lord, I need you right now!" I said to myself, but I was still unable to speak. I was trying to turn my head, swing my arms, and kick my feet, fighting for my life, trying to get away, and finally, I was able to call out, "JESUS!"

At that time, I would always wake up after I called on Jesus. Then I would ask the Lord to watch over me and to bless my family, friends, and neighbors and their neighbors, friends, and families. I'm not exactly sure what the dreams meant, but after thinking about them, my take on them is that my demons were low self-esteem, addictions, and lust of the flesh, and that no matter how bad a situation may be, even when it seems like troubles are coming at you from every side, that if you would have faith and call on Jesus, He will bring you out.

I'm sure there may be others who could understand the dreams better, and if God is willing, maybe one day I will also, or maybe it's just the way I understand it now.

GOD WORKS IN MYSTERIOUS WAYS

Thinking back on some of my darkest days when I was getting high and living in a vacant building. I would go to work not to support my daughter or pay rent but to support my addictions. Every payday, I would lie to myself, saying, "This payday will be different. This time I will give my daughter some money and put some aside for this and that." But things would always turn out the same.

After working forty hours, I would decide that I deserved to relax a while before taking care of business. I would only drink a few beers and smoke one rock. I would take care of other things later. Well, a few hours and a few $100 later, I would be broke and depressed in a dark vacant building looking out the window, thinking, "Man I've messed up again. Lord, please help me."

Although I would spend most of my money on drugs and alcohol, God gave me the mind to spend $10 a week on a prepaid phone, which I would need later for an important call. (God was mysteriously working all the while I thought I was doing something by keeping minutes on my phone.) I tried to stop doing drugs on my own and told myself that I could handle a few drinks. It would work for a while, but a few drinks would always lead to just one hit with my beer, and then just one more and another until I was broke again.

At the end of May 2006, I decided I needed help with my addictions, so I went to a rehab center to ask for help and was told that there was no room at that time. So I went back to the vacant building. About a week later, I told my sister I had tried to get into rehab and was turned away because there was no room. It turns out she used to work for the man who was in charge of the center and had just spoken to him recently. Again, God is doing mysterious work I'm not aware of.

Anyway, she gave me his phone number. A few days later, I was getting high alone in the vacant building and started having chest pains again. So I got down on my knees holding my chest and said, "Lord, you told me if I needed you that you would be there for me. I've been praying for years, and I'm going to keep praying until you answer me."

I then remembered the phone number my sister gave me and decided to call him. I told him I needed help and that I tried to get into their program but was turned away. He asked if anyone took contact information from me, and I told him no. He mentioned that someone should have, and he gave me a name and a number to call. I called the number and was asked who gave me the number. I answered and was asked for contact information.

About five minutes later, God answered, and I received a phone call saying a bed was available. I can only thank God for allowing me to keep minutes on my phone and for using that rehab center as part of my deliverance from drugs and alcohol after thirty years of being addicted. I pray that He continues to work on me so that I can be a blessing to others.

I'm a sinner in recovery that use to be an addict. I only thank God for sending His Son to pay for my deliverance from addictions.

LORD, WHO AM I?

Lord, who am I
That you would love
Enough to send your Son

As if I was important
As if I mattered
As if I was someone

Lord, who am I
That you would watch over me
As I went through my test

Always by my side
Never late with a delivery
Of a way out of my mess

Lord, who am I
That you would stand by
And watch me as I smoked crack

Not there to judge
But to only show love
While asking, "Are you done with that?"

And when I said yes
Lord, I need your help
You were already reaching out your hand

You said, I was always here
Welcome home, my child
You're down, let me help you stand

Lord, who am I
That you will never leave me
Even when I was wrong

The Lord said, You are my child
That was once lost
And I sent my Son to bring you home.

Written by Anonymous Sinner

GOING THROUGH THE 12 STEPS

When I first arrived at the rehab center, I felt a sense of relief. Although I have always kept pretty much to myself and I definitely did not like speaking in front of groups, now I would have to live and speak about personal things in a group setting. I have always been a quiet person, and I still do not even talk much around my family, but I was sick and tired of being sick and tired, and I was grateful for a chance to get help.

I had heard that the first thirty days would be the most important and the hardest, but I also knew that I had people praying for me, giving me more hope. I was taught and believed God's Word when He said that **"where ever there where 2 or more people gathered in agreement in His name that He would be there also" (Matthew 18:20).**

After getting high for the most of my life (thirty years), I had come to the realization that I needed help, and I was now on my way to becoming drug- and alcohol-free. Although in the past I never imagined living without my beer, after failing several attempts to give up drugs and keep the alcohol, I had to stop lying to myself. I had to give them both up. There was also no doubt in my mind that this would not be an easy task. If it were easy to overcome addictions, then selling drugs and alcohol would not be a multibillion-dollar business.

No matter how much some people may pretend like their drug and alcohol use isn't a problem and that they just like spending all their money partying and getting high, fact is, no one wants to be an addict. Growing up, being an addict was never a subject to choose from for Career Day. Most addicts just accept that they are because society tells them that they always will be that way once they become addicted.

Once I was in treatment, I learned that for me drinking was a trigger that always led me to smoking crack. Since one addiction was a trigger for another addiction, I had no choice but to give it all up. This was something that I had to do for myself, and I was also praying that getting clean would help me and my daughter's relationship get better.

The Salvation Army's Harbor Light Center is where God placed me to receive some of my treatment. The center allowed me to draw support off others who were trying to recover. I also spoke with others who were no longer using and now had become counselors. It was where I would learn about the 12 steps and the importance of taking things one day at a time.

Some days were much harder than others, but each day I stayed clean was an important accomplishment. Another day, I had pissed the devil off. After about a week without self-medicating, I started to feel the effects of having no drugs or alcohol to numb my body. I started feeling aches and pains that I normally did not feel. A few days, my side would bother me some and then my leg would hurt, but it was no big deal, I considered myself blessed if this was my withdrawal symptoms.

I had a somewhat high tolerance for pain, so it was no problem. I had felt worst. I was the guy who had gotten hit by a car, got up, and walked away. I was a macho man! A couple of more days went by without me self-medicating, and then my tooth started to ache.

And then there was a change. It seemed as if I had changed from Macho Man to Soft Sally within the blink of an eye.

The center did not allow us to keep any kind of drugs, not even aspirin, and the counselors would pass medications out to us when needed every four hrs. Problem was that the aspirin seemed to wear off every three hours, so I had to suffer for an hour several times a day until I got my tooth pulled about a week later. This was about week 3, when my tooth started hurting.

After taking some aspirin at night, I was able to get a couple of hours of rest, and then I would wake up in pain again and had to just lie there and wait until I could get some more aspirin.

I'd be lying in bed rocking, saying to myself that I'm more than a conqueror, I'm more than a conqueror, I'm not Soft Sally, I'm not Soft Sally. Lord, help me make it through this.

Then the devil would speak to me, saying, "Man, this makes no sense for you to be just lying here in pain. You're a grown man, and they won't even let you keep some aspirin? That's messed up. This isn't jail, and no one is making you stay here. You can walk away from this center now and go get you a drink and a pair of pliers if you need to. It's been a while since you've had a good night's sleep. Why put up with this when you don't have to? You should just leave because this is ridiculous. A grown man, yet you have to wait on someone else to give you permission to take some aspirin."

Then I would hear the Lord saying, "THE DEVIL IS A LIE. YOU ARE MORE THAN A CONQUEROR. JUST HOLD ON FOR A WHILE LONGER."

The 12 Steps (As written by the NA, followed by how I personally got through them and continue to do so)

1. WE ADMITTED THAT WE WRE POWERLESS OVER OUR ADDICTION, THAT OUR LIVES HAD BECOME UNMANAGEABLE.

    This was a step I had already accomplished, and I'd already heard about the concept. Basically, in order to deal with a problem, you first have to admit that there is one.

2. WE CAME TO BELIEVE THAT A POWER GREATER THAN OURSELVES COULD RESTORE US TO SANITY.

    I was taught as a child that God had power over all things and that through Christ all things were possible.

3.   WE MADE A DECISION TO TURN OUR WILL AND OUR LIVES OVER TO THE CARE OF GOD AS WE UNDERSTOOD HIM.

   After trying and failing to get over my addictions on my own, I got sick and tired of being sick and tired. My willpower was not strong enough, so I prayed that God would help me. I knew that in my weakness that God was still strong. For this problem, I had to let go and let God.

4.   WE MADE A SEARCHING AND FEARLESS MORAL INVENTORY OF OURSELVES.

   While in the rehab center, I was able to listen to others whom I was able to relate to, and at times, I was also able to speak one-on-one with counselors, some of which had used drugs and alcohol in their past. It gave me time to reflect on some of my experiences as a child looking for more attention from my dad and trying to find somewhere to fit in. Experiences and decisions that led to the evolvement of my addictions.

5.   WE ADMITTED TO GOD, TO OURSELVES, AND TO ANOTHER HUMAN BEING THE EXACT NATURE OF OUR WRONGS.

   After reflecting on some of my past experiences, I had to admit to myself that although others around me were not perfect, neither was I. Some of my bad experiences were do to the choices that I made using the free will given to me by God. Everything wrong in my life was not someone else's fault. I had to own up to my mistakes.

6.   WE WERE ENTIRELY READY TO HAVE GOD REMOVE ALL THESE DEFECTS OF CHARACTER.

   After owning up to my mistakes, I realized that I needed to stop lying to myself. There were things about me that I needed to change, and I couldn't do them without Gods help. I also understood that I did not become the way I was overnight and that I wouldn't completely change overnight, but through Christ, I could change.

7. WE HUMBLY ASKED HIM TO REMOVE OUR SHORTCOMINGS.

For me, I had to accept Christ as my savior. I prayed for a better understanding of the Bible and that God would remove more of my will and replace it with more of His.

8. WE MADE A LIST OF ALL PERSONS WE HAD HARMED, AND BECAME WILLING TO MAKE AMENDS TO THEM ALL.

I had to learn to forgive myself for the mistakes that I had made and accept the fact that others were affected by my actions and deserved an apology also.

9. WE MADE DIRECT AMENDS TO SUCH PEOPLE WHEREVER POSSIBLE, EXCEPT WHEN TO DO SO WOULD INJURE THEM OR OTHERS.

I asked God and people who were effected by my mistakes for forgiveness.

10. WE CONTINUED TO TAKE PERSONAL INVENTORY AND WHEN WE WERE WRONG PROMPTLY ADMITTED IT.

I continue to own up to my mistakes when I make them, and I continue to seek God in order to better myself.

11. WE SOUGHT THROUGH PRAYER AND MEDITATION TO IMPROVE OUR CONSCIOUS CONTACT WITH GOD AS WE UNDERSTOOD HIM, PRAYING ONLY FOR KNOWLEDGE OF HIS WILL FOR US AND THE POWER TO CARRY THAT OUT.

I continue to ask God for a better understanding of His Word and His will for me. I started going back to church praying also for a change in my thought process. There had been a change in me, but I still needed more work. I knew that I couldn't change, if I continued to think the same, it would take time for my thought process to change and my change would not be possible without God.

12. HAVING HAD A SPIRITUAL AWAKENING AS A RESULT OF THESE STEPS, WE TRIED TO CARRY THIS MESSAGE TO ADDICTS, AND TO PRACTICE THESE PRINCIPLES IN ALL OUR AFFAIRS.

After receiving help, out of gratitude, I will continue to give thanks and grow while practicing what I've learned and studying God's Word. I will also try to help others by spreading a message of hope through my testimony.

BY HIS WOUNDS WE ARE HEALED

"By His wounds we are healed" are some powerful words. A lot of people fail to realize how powerful they are. Some of man's words are powerful too. Some of them are "Addicts suffer from a disease for which there's no cure," and plenty of people continue to tell themselves that they're addicts. By giving those words power, they give their addictions power over themselves instead of taking power over their addictions. ADDICTS SUFFER FROM A DISEASE IN WHICH MAN HAS NO CURE!

We all need to learn to take more control over the words we speak. To stay encouraged and try to keep negative words off our tongues. Speak positive words for a positive life. God's words tell us that we can do all things through Christ. So if we have faith, thank God for what He's done, pray for better things to come and for strength through Christ, we can overcome anything negative in our lives.

Jesus performed miracles in His Father's name throughout the Bible. There's not one scripture that says Jesus touched the blind and gave them partial sight or that He laid hands on the deaf and they were able to hear a little out of one ear. God is not capable of halfway curing someone. Only man has those capabilities. God has a miracle tailor-made just for you, and it's yours to claim if you would have faith.

The Bible tells us in **Mathew 13:58 where Jesus did not perform many miracles because the people there didn't have enough faith**. Man's words: "Addicts suffer from a disease for which there's no cure are words from men with no faith." God's words **in Isaiah**

53:5 says, "But He was pierced for our transgressions, He was crushed for our iniquities, the punishment that brought us peace was upon Him, and by HIS WOUNDS WE ARE HEALED."

God gave us all free will, so it's up to you to decide which words will have more power in your life, man's words or Gods words.

I am a sinner in recovery, that use to be an addict, but by HIS WOUNDS, I AM HEALED!

SPREADING THE
MESSAGE OF HOPE

How can I practice what I've learned and help other addicts? Though it's true that God has delivered me from my addictions, I know that I'm still a sinner in recovery. Though I no longer use drugs and alcohol, I still had part of the same mind-set that I had while I was using.

I didn't agree with everything that I had heard while in treatment, but I believed that God delivered me to give me a testimony. I also knew that a testimony that wasn't shared was not the right way to give thanks to God or beneficial to others. Therefore, I could not carry a message of hope to addicts by not sharing my story.

There was no way I could give hope to someone who felt hopeless without sharing some good news. News of how through Christ I overcame something they can relate to. Personally, like many others, I'm not real comfortable with public speaking, but I believe that from time to time everyone needs some kind of encouragement and support from someone whom they feel understands them and that they can relate to.

I've started a Christian-based online community for sinners in recovery (Anonymous Sinner.com @ www.AnonymousSinner.com) as a way to help carry a message of hope to others through prayer, shared testimonies, fellowship, and through encouraging the development of a personal relationship with God.

I was also fully aware of the fact that I could not spread the message of hope by hanging out at the club or liquor store with active addicts every day. I remembered a statement I heard while in treatment that if you keep hanging at the barbershop, sooner or later you're going to get a haircut.

So there was no way for me to spread hope by hanging around the dope sets and liquor stores because sooner or later I would be tempted, and I could never give hope to an addict by relapsing. I also remembered that I received some hope by just seeing a sober friend from time to time who stopped just to say, "Hello, I'm still clean, God bless you and keep your head up." Just by seeing him, I saw that God was still able and that the blood still worked.

TO SPREAD HOPE, I COULDN'T BE ASHAMED OF MY TESTIMONY

> **"Therefore do not become ashamed of the witness about our Lord, neither of me a prisoner for his sake, but take your part in suffering evil for the good news according to the power of God." (2 Timothy 1:8)**

God is truly a good God and worthy to be praised. A lot of people say that they agree with that, yet they won't testify. We as a people have gotten so caught up on the opinions of others that we tend to hold back on our praise. In private, we thank God that we no longer use drugs, steal, or sell our bodies. In public, it's like, "Lord, I thank you for what you've done for me, but I can't tell anyone what you've done for me because I don't want them to look at me different."

Fact is, God allowed you to go through things, and He brought you out to show that He is God, the highest of higher powers. In doing so, He wants you to be a light so that others can see His grace and mercy through you.

You may be asking yourself why I am using the name an Anonymous Sinner if I'm not ashamed of my testimony. I chose to use that pen name with the hopes of being more relatable to more readers in which case my testimony will reach more people.

Another reason why I created the website Anonymous Sinners is that I also understand that for some people the right words may not always come to them while in front of other people. So my website will be a place for people to gather their thoughts and then share their testimony.

I truly believe that our testimonies have the power to put a spotlight on the fact that we can overcome anything through Christ. Some people are still suffering through the same things you did, and they're looking for a glimpse of hope, which they may find in something that you shared with them.

Yes, they may believe in God, but their faith isn't strong because to them God may seem to be too far out of reach. They may be in a dark place where they feel like there's no hope just because it has been too long since something good has happened in their lives. This is where our testimonies come in. We need to be on our jobs of promoting Christ.

Through our testimonies, we can bring God up close and personal to those who are in need of something to brighten up their lives. The hope is that if one person can overcome something through Christ, then so can they. We need to go to work and be a light for our Lord so that others can see His mercy and grace through us. After all that He's done for you and your family, isn't God worthy of a testimony?

If I Don't, Maybe Someone Else Will

Will I offer encouragement to someone in need
To help their faith grow, will I plant the seed
If I don't, maybe someone else will

Will I offer shelter to someone in the rain
Even when for myself, there's nothing to gain
If I don't, maybe someone else will

Will I give to a man standing on the street
A little of what I have so that he can eat
If I don't, maybe someone else will

Will I extend my friendship to someone alone
Knowing that they're new to a place, will I make them feel at home
If I don't, maybe someone else will

Will I pray for others even when they don't ask me to
Will I make it to heaven by putting off what God wants me to do
If I don't, maybe someone else will

Knowing Jesus died for you,
How do you feel
Would you be the same if Christ had the attitude
IF I DON'T, MAYBE SOMEONE ELSE WILL

Written by Anonymous Sinner

WE'RE NOT PERFECT, BUT THROUGH CHRIST, WE CAN BETTER OURSELVES

Sometimes, we all just need a place to vent, pray, and have others join us in prayer without the feeling of being judged but with the feeling of being understood and cared for. Some may even feel that because of their past that no one cares. The devil has lied to them so much that they start to believe they just don't matter that much. He has even convinced many to admit to themselves they are hopeless. That they are who they are and that they could never change.

It is true that you will always be you, but through Christ, you can change. No one was born walking and talking, and although you're the same person you were at birth, you changed as you grew. As long as we live, each of us has potential for growth.

The question is whether or not we will allow ourselves to. We can grow by performing a self-inventory, owning up to our short-comings, and, most importantly, taking time to develop a personal relationship with God and asking Him for a better understanding of His will for us. Then we can pray for the wisdom and strength to carry it out.

THE SERENITY PRAYER

God, grant me the Serenity
To accept the things I cannot change,
Courage to change the things I can,
And Wisdom to know the difference.
Living one day at a time,
Enjoying one moment at a time,
Accepting hardship as the pathway to peace.
Taking, as He did, this sinful world as it is,
Not as I would have it.
Trusting that He will make all things right
if I surrender to His will.
That I may be reasonably happy in this life,
And supremely happy with Him forever in the next.
Amen.

Attributed to Reinhold Neibuhr

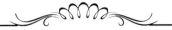

AND THE TESTS GO ON

I am now and will always be a sinner in recovery until Christ returns to recover me. As long as we live, each of us will be tested. Through addictions, I was tested, and now that I've been delivered from drugs and alcohol through Christ, I still continue to be tested in life. The devil does not want me to receive my blessings, so he keeps trying to throw me off track.

I've struggled with issues of lust trying to fulfill a physical need and, other times, with violent thoughts because I felt as if someone was trying to punk me. I reacted this way due to my worldly mind-set. Through Christ, I've realized that I do not have to prey on women with low self-esteem because of my issues, nor do I have to act ignorant just because I'm qualified.

Understanding that there will always be some kind of test, I had to learn to identify some of my personal-blessing blockers and issues (through self-inventory), and when I'm tempted, I just have to learn to let go quicker and let God.

I'm still a work in progress, and I need a lot of work while I am still rehabbing my mind-set. Please pray for this sinner in recovery.

While rehabbing my mind-set, I had to start throwing out some of my old ways of thinking. I had to start owning up to some of my faults, and I needed to remove some of my blessing blockers (excuses). Everything bad that happened to me was not someone else's fault. There were times when I decided not to go to work or pay a bill so that I could get high. Other times, people tried to tell me right and I decided to do wrong. No one owed me anything. I owed it to myself to do better, and to my God for giving me a way to fight my temptations even when I never deserved it, and sometimes, I would not even accept them.

During a self-inventory, I realized that my excuses were my main blessing blockers. I needed to stop making excuses for what was wrong. I had to stop worrying about what others had and learn to be grateful for what I had. I also needed to start making more of an effort to change myself for the better. But most of all, I needed to accept the fact that everything was not about me. It was about learning to focus more on God and His Word. Only then would my life truly change for the better.

> **"But remember that the temptations that come into your life is no different from what others experience. And God is faithful. He will keep the temptation from becoming so strong that you can't stand up against it. When you are tempted, He will show you a way out so that you will not give in to it" (1 Corinthians 10:13).**

NOTE: NOWHERE IN THAT SCRIPTURE DID IT STATE THAT EVERYTHING WILL BE EASY. It just states that God will show you a way out when you are tempted. It's up to you to decide which way to go.

Why Can't I Be Blessed

Why can't I be blessed?
Others around me have a job, a house, a car
I could've done that job better than them
But the bus stop was too far

Why can't I be blessed?
It seems your love for them is greater
I know there are things required of me
And I will get to them later

Why can't I be blessed?
I'm a good person, Lord, can't you see my heart?
I know I should pay my tides and offerings
Once I get more money, I'll start

Why can't I be blessed?
Do I not matter, is everyone more important than me?
I will pray later when things slow down
Right now, I'm kind of busy

The Lord said
I blessed you this morning
When I woke you with a touch, because I found the time
I blessed you before you were even born
With blood from the Only Begotten Son of mine
I blessed you with free will
And ability to do what you can do
And yet still you are too busy to even say, Lord, thank you
I've blessed you in many ways
One is to claim things in my name
But to shout "I am your Lord" to the world
You seem to be ashamed

But when it's all said and done
Time for me you have none
You won't seek my face or call my name
I have more blessings for you
But there's something that you must do
You must realize:
"I AM THE LORD YOUR GOD"
AND I AM GOD ALONE!
IT'S ABOUT ME
IT'S NOT ABOUT YOU

Written by Anonymous Sinner

YOU'RE ALREADY PREPARED

Is there something you feel like God has put on your heart to do but you're not quite sure how to go about doing it? You keep being led to do something, but instead of acting on it, you block your blessing by asking, "Lord, why me?"

Why not you? If the Lord has given you a task, then you're already prepared to do it. Don't misunderstand me; there will always be something to overcome, but as a child of God, you are more than a conqueror. So when you come up to an obstacle, keep your faith, stand on it, and press on.

God gave me the idea for a website. My plan was to have it up and running by August 2014 but that didn't work out. I was able to get two versions of the site up by September, but that also didn't work, yet I pressed on to site 3 and a new name for it.

I pressed on because this was an assignment God had given to me. I also had to learn that my plan wasn't the most important but God's was. All I had to do was ask for guidance, be still, and wait on the Lord.

I had to learn a lesson to better prepare me for the site. Just like going to school, in life, you go through a series of lessons to prepare you for what's to come. I believe that God calls each of us for assignments designed specifically for us based on our life experiences. However, some of us make excuses not to except them, such as, "I'm not qualified."

I'd be the first to admit that I'm not a public speaker, and I don't believe that I'm qualified to be a preacher at this time, but only God knows my future. I can't quote Bible scriptures off the top of my head, but I believe God's Word. I am just a blessed sinner in recovery who's praying for guidance while trying to be a better man and do the assignment given to me the best I can. This is an assignment that I was prepared for through my life experiences, and I know that what I'm going through now will prepare me for what's next.

So do not turn away from the assignment God has given you thinking that you're not qualified. God does not just give assignments to the qualified according to their education, He uses everyday people. That makes it easier for us to relate to each other.

Once you accept the assignment, continue to pray for guidance, wait on the Lord, and then the Holy Spirit will qualify you. Just remember that whatever assignment God has given you, you're already prepared to do it. You just need to activate your faith.

ACTIVATE YOUR FAITH

I come to you in the name of our Father in heaven as a person who's trying to be a better man by learning to exercise my faith more. I know that it's by God's grace that I still have life. Although I do not know God's complete purpose for me, I'm learning how to pray better. Not just to ask God for what I want and need but, more importantly, to ask God for what He wants from me.

In the process, I still sometimes have to remind myself that I need to give more control to God instead of trying to run things myself. I'm also slowly developing better listening skills. After all, prayer is just having a conversation with God, and in any good conversation, there's talking and listening.

I've been asking God for guidance, and I've started reading His Word trying to get a better understanding of it. I also know that God wants us to be productive and put in some work. To be productive, we must have faith along with works.

> **"Of what benefit is it, my brothers, if a certain one says he has faith but he does not have works? That faith can not save him can it? If a brother or a sister is naked and lacking food sufficient for the day, yet a certain one of you says to them: Go in peace, keep warm and well fed, but you do not give them the necessities for their body, of what benefit is it. Thus too faith, if it does not have works is dead in itself." (James 2:14–17)**

God gave us all a measure of faith. Have faith in God's Word, and take time to read it for yourself even if it's only reading along with the pastor at church as he is teaching. Also share the good news about our Father in heaven. Visit the sick. Invite someone to church, Bible study, or maybe a Christian website (hint, hint: www. AnonymousSinner.com), share your testimony, and help someone in need because faith apart from works is inactive.

It is up to each of us to activate our own faith. We activate it by trusting in God's Word in spite of our situation. We allow it to grow by putting in work, allowing the light of Jesus to shine through us by our words and actions.

Today, be encouraged, and offer encouragement to others. Don't think for a moment that you're not important enough to make a difference. God can use you as you are right now. Go to Him today with your concerns, put your trust in Him, and then go and tell someone how good God is. Wherever you are in life, get on your mark, get set, ACTIVATE YOUR FAITH. Once it has been activated, you will find that the Lord is all you need.

The Lord Is

The Lord is the reason I have life,
He died so that I may live.
The Lord is the author of my story,
He gave me a testimony to give.
The Lord is my companion,
with Him I'm never alone.
The Lord is my guide,
leading me to my Father's home.
The Lord is my sponsor,
and He's always within reach.
The Lord is my instructor,
always willing and able to teach.
The Lord is my sight,
seeing far beyond what I can see.
The Lord is my nourishment,
providing food for me to eat.
The Lord is my strength,
for He is strong when I am weak.
The Lord is not a man,
His promises He will keep.
The Lord is my gardener,
allowing me to grow as a mustard seed.
The Lord is my shepherd,
and I have all that I need.

Written by Anonymous Sinner

CHANGING THE MIND-SET OF

A SINNER IN RECOVERY

"HIS WORD WILL CHANGE YOU FROM THE INSIDE OUT. LET THE SPIRIT CHANGE YOUR WAY OF THINKING AND MAKE YOU INTO A NEW PERSON."
(Ephesians 4: 23–24)

I can remember my dad's most famous line that he used to tell all his children, and it was "Stop and think." That would be a phrase that I would have to improve on after treatment because my ways of thinking were not always very good; therefore, I would need to learn to "stop and rethink" before reacting to some thoughts.

Over the years, before I started and while I was getting high, every once in a while I would attend church or have someone on the street pray for me. I would accept Christ as my savior again and ask for forgiveness of my sins again. I had always believed in God and that Christ died for me so that my life would be better, but after prayer and asking for forgiveness, I would always go back to the same old routine again. My mind-set was set for the ways of the world because I had allowed the ways of the world to take my focus off God and put it all on what I want right now.

I had fallen for the devil's lie that life was too short and that I deserved to party and enjoy myself while I was alive. From years of unintentionally programming my mind by watching TV, reading things other than the Bible, listening to worldly music, and not going to church regularly, I came to the wrong conclusion of how to enjoy life based on the ways of the world. I was grateful for the grace God had shown me, and through Christ, I had recovered from my addictions.

Though I had become a new creature, I was still a sinner in recovery, and there were changes that still needed to be made. Changes that would not be made overnight. I was still a work in progress, and I needed a lot of work. I had to learn how to reset my mind-set as my mind-set went through rehab. To do that, I had to start taking more focus off the ways of the world and put more focus on God by studying His Word, attending church regularly, and taking time to develop a personal relationship with Him.

While receiving treatment for my addictions, I received an extra bonus. Somewhere along my treatment, I started liking myself. Although I've always loved myself, I can't remember when during my years of confusion that I stopped liking myself. Certainly it was during the times when I would constantly disappoint myself by spending all my money getting high without even having a place to live of my own. I'm not even exactly sure when I started liking myself again; it just kind of crept up on me during my treatment.

One day, I just woke up liking myself again because I had a daughter who was starting to talk to me and a few dollars in my pocket from the day before.

The exact day may have been around the time shortly after my first day pass after my first thirty days in treatment. I remember on my first pass I was going through my old neighborhood and I had seen a guy who was on his way to get high. We had seen each other from time to time over the years in various spots where we went to get high, and he never offered me any dope before.

However, on this day, he offered me some (that's just how the devil works, he's always looking for ways to throw you off track), and I can remember telling the guy, "No, I don't mess around anymore."

Listen here, listen here. That sounded so nice I had to repeat it to myself as I walked off feeling a since of pride and gratitude: "No, I don't mess around anymore." You can tell me that God isn't good, but I won't believe you because I know better. If God would give me the strength to say no once I know that He would do it again, and He has over the years as I ran across people I use to get high with. Without knowing it, I may even be giving hope to others the way an old friend gave hope to me. I pray that I am and continue to do so.

After receiving and leaving treatment, I was a new creature. I was not perfect, but I was new even though I still needed to be made over again. I no longer wanted to use drugs and alcohol, but I still had a lust for the flesh. I was going to church most Sundays but not every Sunday, and through the week, my mind was still on worldly things.

At the time, I had no place of my own, and I was staying with a family member who was trying to be a crack dealer. Sometimes he would allow customers to come in and get high. To avoid being around people smoking crack, I would leave. I had a car at the time and I would go for rides around town. Most of the times, I would go by the houses of girls I used to get high with, or I would go down the streets where prostitutes were, and I would spend time with them in order to satisfy my flesh.

I knew that I was supposed to be carrying a message of hope to other addicts and that what I was doing was wrong, but the flesh wanted what the flesh wanted. My mind-set told me that there was no reason why a grown man should go more than a week without sex. It was just too easy to come by, especially with a girl with an active addiction and my unwillingness to just "stop and rethink," that I could have used this opportunity to show someone that they mattered.

This was something I had to continue praying on, and after a while, I started to feel guilty about what I was doing. Later, God blessed me with my own apartment. I stopped running the streets as if I was attending a clearance sale at Prostitutes R Us, but I still entertained women who got high. Again, I did not allow them to smoke dope around me, but I would buy them drinks while they were with me. Others I gave a few dollars to go with to buy the drugs of their choice.

How could I be grateful for my deliverance and still support other addicts? Even though some of the girls sometimes said that they needed a few dollars for other things, I still knew they were lying. They wanted a few dollars for drugs. I was not new to how life was on the streets for someone with an addiction, and what the money was used for didn't matter as much as it should have to me. My main concern was that my need was taken care of and that she got high after I left.

AnonymousSinner.com

There's an old saying that "an idle mind is the devil's workshop." I needed to find something to do with my time now that I wasn't getting high anymore. Something to help me with my lustful mind-set and give me a way to carry a message of hope to other addicts.

God gave me the idea for my website, and I started it. It would be a Christian-based online website for people who may have or may still be dealing with addictions as well as other life issues.

The goal was to create a site that was more than just social media but something that would become life media where people could go to get support 24-7 without feeling judged while also helping them develop a personal relationship with God. I knew that only through Christ and through me taking time to develop a personal relationship with God is what would save me from me.

I also knew that, like me, many people were not comfortable speaking in public, so this site would be a way for them to say what was on their minds to others who understood them and would lift their names up in prayer.

It took a few tries to get it going, but it's now up and running. Before I got the site together and before I met the blessing that is now in my life, sometimes I still would have girls over whom I called my friends, and later I would feel a since of guilt after spending time with them. (God was working and continues to work on me.)

How could I call myself a friend? I would tell them that I was grateful for God delivering me from my addictions while they sat drinking a beer that I'd bought them. A true friend would not offer drugs or alcohol to someone they knew was dealing with an addiction or take advantage of someone dealing with issues of low self-esteem.

I realized I needed and still need more than just church on Sundays, but I needed to touch basis with God daily in order to improve my personal relationship with Him. Though the price for my sins have been paid for in full, I am still a sinner in recovery as the changes in me are still changing as the development of my personal relationship with God continues.

Praise God I'm doing much better now. The rehabbing of my mind-set continues. I'm grateful that me and my daughter are talking or texting each other every week (when she used to act like I bothered her by breathing). I was even blessed to walk her down the aisle when she got married, when I wasn't even invited to her high school graduation. I'm also learning to choose better ways to go when I'm tempted by the flesh or other worldly things most of the time.

Everything is not perfect, but I know that I've come a long way and that things are much better than they used to be. At times, I feel a little lonely, but that only tells me that I need to find something more to do with my time, and I trust God that I will find me a life-long Christian companion.

I still need prayer because I realize lust is a weapon formed against me. Though I still have lustful thoughts from time to time, through going to church regularly and from the studying of the Word, I'm learning to **"bring every thought into captivity" (2 Corinthians 10:5)**.

If I'm walking down the street and see an attractive lady, I may catch myself imagining how nice it would be to spend time with her. Then I have to stop and repent and rethink: "Lord, help me, and please forgive me now. I know that I was wrong for the thoughts I had. Please help me not to mess up the blessing I have for a chance of losing her to gain what could just be a headache."

I sometimes have to do a moral self-inventory and check myself, asking for strength to bring my thoughts into captivity while also sometimes praying for some ladies that one day they may not feel the need to dress that way to get the attention of a man. Of course, I do not do that as quickly as I should all the time, but I'm still a work in progress.

I NOW KNOW THAT A LITTLE BIT OF PLEASURE CAN LEAD TO A WHOLE LOT OF PAIN BEFORE THE FLAME. If the humidity in St. Louis gets to be too much at times for me, I'm sure I won't like hell. So I will continue to develop a better personal relationship with God by going to church with the lady I was blessed to meet and trying to get a better understanding of His Word. I will also continue to do a self-inventory and own up to my mistakes and repent when I'm wrong daily while I'm learning to change my mindset. Yesterday's repentance was for yesterday. Right now, for me, nine times out of nine, I will still need forgiveness today, because I am a sinner in recovery.

**"I am being transformed by a renewed mind."
(Romans 12:2)**

I Repented Yesterday

I repented yesterday
So for now it's all good
I heard someone was going to step to me wrong
It's okay, I wish he would

I repented yesterday
Do I really need to do it again
God knows I have a good heart
And I don't mean to sin

I repented yesterday
But today I called someone out of their name
They know I wasn't serious
And that it was all just fun and games

I repented yesterday
For my words and my thoughts
Since no one was hurt
Was anything really lost

I repented yesterday
For my attitude and behavior
I know I need to work on them both
I will sooner or later

I repented yesterday
Why make everything a big deal
For no one is perfect
Like they say, let's keep it real

I repented yesterday
Though I don't have much cash flow
I bought something for myself
Instead of planting a seed to sow

I repented yesterday
Lord, Your grace is still needed
So I repent again today
While things remain a secret

I repented yesterday
Before all things are exposed
I ask for forgiveness now
And that you make friends out of my foes

I repented yesterday
Through Christ I learned how
For my wrong thoughts, actions, and words since
Lord, please forgive me now

Written by Anonymous Sinner

The World in Me

The world in me
The world in me
Its presence is not as strong

The world in me
Lord, as I seek Thee
More and more is gone

The world in me
To which I once was blind
Now I'm starting to see

I was losing to sin
But through Christ now I win
Oh, how I love Thee

The world in me
Lord, I thank Thee
For my eyes have started to open

I pray you take it away
So my eyes can stay
On the path that you have chosen

The world in me
Through substance abuse
To the dark, Lord, you brought light

So that I could shine
Through no power of mine
For Jesus is the light

The world in me
Lord, take it away
Make me over, completely new

So that others can see
The Christ in me
Not the world like they used too

Written by Anonymous Sinner

IT'S YOUR ETERNITY,
IT'S YOUR CHOICE

Life is full of choices. I would go as far as to say that most of your life is spent making choices. Wouldn't you agree?

Early in my life, I made a really bad choice to hang with people who used drugs and alcohol. As the years went by, I continued to make a lot of bad choices. I thank God for my mother who used to take me to church and impounded in my head that Jesus loved me, died for me, and that no matter what I did He would forgive me if I repented. I also learned that He was the only way to our Father in heaven.

Although most of my choices weren't the brightest, I did make a few good ones. I made the choice to pray for deliverance from my addictions. I also made the choice to ask Him for a better understanding of His Word, and that He would teach me to listen for His voice.

I'm now making a choice to get to know Him better. To know God personally is very important to me. A lot of people know of Him but don't really know Him. Yes, I know of Him sending Jesus to die for me. Yes, I know that the Father, Son, and the Holy Spirit are as one, but I have to go through the Son to get to the Father.

I know of the woman with issues of blood in Luke 8:43–47 touching the Lord's garment and being healed. I know of Jesus using some of His spit mixed with dirt to give a blind man sight in John 9:6–7. But even more important, I know I do not want to be like the people in Matthew 8:22–23, when the Lord tells them, "I never knew you. Get away from me."

To secure my place in eternity, I'm choosing to get to know Him by taking time to study His Word for myself. Do you really know Him? Also, where do you choose to spend your eternity? Smoking or nonsmoking? The smoking will be burning in hell or the nonsmoking in a room prepared by Jesus in His Father's house.

Repent for your sins today, find a good church to join, and accept Christ as your savior. It's your eternity, it's your choice, and I encourage you to choose Christ.

Water in My Eyes

I was taught a man should be strong
Not letting his feelings show
Even though nothing's wrong
Sometimes tears start to flow

It was something I heard
While the preacher taught the Word
That allowed me to clearly see

Through the scripture he chose
A truth was exposed
God cared for me

Am I truly blessed
The answer is yes
This much I know is true

That life is full of tests and according to your faith
What He's done for others
He'll do for you

There's a cure for addictions "in the blood"
It's always been there, in plain sight
At first I couldn't find it, in God's Word
Because I wasn't reading it right

So I prayed for a better understanding
And God answered my prayers
He sent books to read and preachers to teach
Just to show He cared

That I was in a bad situation
For the devil had me bound
I was once lost to addictions
Because of God's grace, I've now been found

To God I give praise and thanks
The devil will no longer be my demise
I'm so grateful, there's nothing wrong
I just got WATER IN MY EYES

Written by Anonymous Sinner

This is something I like to share with you that my mother received from someone and shared with me.

God is interested in your spiritual, emotional, and psychological growth and well-being. Knowing who you are in Christ will help you grow and become the overcomer whom God created you to be.

Listed here are several scriptural affirmations based on your life in Christ. Recite these daily until they become a part of your new life and consciousness. Say them aloud where you can hear them.

1. I am a child of God.
2. I am redeemed from the hand of the enemy (Psalm 107:2).
3. I am forgiven (Colossians 1:14).
4. I am saved by grace through faith (Ephesians 2:8).
5. I am justified (Romans 5:1).
6. I am sanctified (1 Corinthians 6:11).
7. I am a new creature (2 Corinthians 5:17).
8. I am partaker of His divine nature (2 Peter 1:4).
9. I am redeemed from the curse of the law (Galatians 3:13).
10. I am delivered from the powers of darkness (Colossians 1:13).
11. I am led by the spirit of God (Romans 8:14).
12. I am kept in safety wherever I go (Psalms 91:11).
13. I am getting all my needs met by Jesus (Philip. 4:19).
14. I am casting all my cares on Jesus (1 Peter 5:7).
15. I am strong in the Lord and the power of His might (Ephesians 6:10).
16. I am doing things through Christ who strengthens me (Philippians 4:13).
17. I am an heir of God and a joint heir with Jesus (Romans 8:17).
18. I am observing and doing the Lord's commandments (Deuteronomy 28:12).
19. I am blessed coming in and going out (Deuteronomy 28:6).
20. I am an inheritor of eternal life (1 John 5:11–12).
21. I am blessed with all spiritual blessings (Ephesians 1:3).
22. I am healed by his stripes (1 Peter 2:24).
23. I am exercising my authority over the enemy (Luke 10:19).
24. I am above only and not beneath (Deuteronomy 28:13).

25. I am more than a conqueror (Romans 8:37).
26. I am establishing God's Word here on earth (Matthew 16:19).
27. I am an overcomer by the blood of the Lamb and the words of my testimony (Revelation 12:11).
28. I am walking by faith and not by sight (2 Corinthians 5:7).
29. I am casting down vain imaginations (2 Corinthians 10:4).
30. I am bringing every thought into captivity (2 Corinthians 10:5).
31. I am being transformed by a renewed mind (Romans 12:1–2).
32. I am a laborer together with God (1 Corinthians 3:9).
33. I am an imitator of Jesus (Ephesians 5:1).
34. I am the light of the world (Matthew 5:14).
35. I am learning truth and that truth makes me free (John 8:32).
36. I am chosen and ordained to bring forth fruit (John15:16).
37. I am a recipient of peace (John 14:27).
38. I am confident of a good work being done in me (Philippians 1:6).

CONFESS WHO YOU ARE IN CHRIST!

Knowing who you are in Christ will change your life dramatically. As you begin to confess these truths daily, your faith will increase and your life will change for the better. You will have health, prosperity (both spiritually and financially), and the abundant life that Jesus came to provide for you (John 10:10).

Try confessing these thirty-eight truths and watch how your life will change for the better! **Faith come by hearing and hearing by the word of God (Romans 10:17).** God bless you.

I do not claim to be a perfect man, but I do claim to be a man in need of prayer as I am a sinner in recovery seeking a better relationship with God. I pray that this book will be a blessing to someone today as they read it and understand that someone understands their struggles, and that they're not alone in the situation they're facing.

I still remember the lady who stopped me when I was on my way to buy some drugs and asked if she could say a prayer for me. She said that she saw that God had a purpose for me. Maybe this book is it, or maybe my website, www.AnonymousSinners.com, or maybe there will be more. I pray that God continues to use me until He uses me up.

May God be given the praise and the glory for what He has done and continues to do in our lives, and may our faith be increased. Please share this book or buy another copy for a friend or loved one who may have or may still be dealing with an addiction so that they may receive a spark of hope, which in return will strengthen their faith. Or just give it to someone who just enjoys good news of what God has done and is doing in the lives of other sinners in recovery.

REMEMBER THAT GOD IS STILL IN THE BLESSING BUSINESS, AND MY PRAYER IS THAT HE CONTINUES TO DO BUSINESS WITH YOU.

To and from Crack to Christ

To and from crack to Christ, throughout my life
God was making moves
In order to learn what was needed
He allowed me to go to school

Through the school of life, I've made mistakes
As I live, I will make more
I pray for an increase in faith
And that God continues to open doors

From the age of twelve to forty-two
My addictions started and evolved
I was living life without a clue
Of how later it would affect my child

Starting to get high so young
Believing that it was cool
Thinking I was so smart, I was dumb
And decided to drop out of school

I wanted to be with my peers
People I thought were my friends
So I smoked weed and drank beer
Trying to just fit in

After years of getting high
Thinking my life was on track
At the age of twenty-five
A "friend" gave me crack

The devil set me up
And caused trouble in my life and home
Because God loved me so much
He never left me alone

I'd made mistakes and I'd fallen
And the devil kicked me while I was down
At times I wanted to give in
As I cried out, "LORD, I NEED YOU NOW"

As I went through my addictions
From alcohol, to weed, to crack
I always knew that God was with me
I owe my mother for that

I remembered the God in me
That my mother told me was there
That the Lord would never forsake me
When needed, He'd always be there

While at my lowest I called out to Jesus
The name above all names
And one second before too late
My Lord and Savior came

So now I'm moving on up
Much further than the East Side
I have a room prepared in my Father's house
Way up in the sky

I can ONLY THANK GOD for His Son
For a way out of my addictions, He paid the price
Like the Jeffersons, I've moved on up
But I moved TO AND FROM CRACK TO CHRIST

Written by Anonymous Sinner

Thank You, Thank You, Thank You

Thank You, Thank You, Thank You
It is hard to express in words for a sinner like me
The appreciation for the grace that I continue to receive
Just to say thank-you is way far below, not enough
Please forgive me for not fully knowing how to show gratefulness for
Your touch

Thank You, Thank You, Thank You again
For Your forgiveness of the mistakes of an imperfect man
For the mistakes I will make today, tomorrow, and in the past
Thank You for the type of forgiveness that will NEVER BE
SURPASSED

Lord, I know that I am not worthy of the love that has been shown
But I pray that you continue to mold me as one of Your own
Throughout this walk, open my eyes so that I can see the steps
For those hidden in darkness, send an angel to push me right or left

For sinners in recovery, I know the list goes on and on
If it had not been for Jesus, all hope would have been gone
So, Lord, I want to thank You, for Your work with me is not done
And for all that You love, You still have time for one-on-one

Thank You, Thank You, Thank You
For loving me so much
That You allow me in my darkest hours
To still feel Your touch

Thank You, Thank You, Thank You
For each step You allow me to complete
Give me the strength to keep moving forward
As You also guide my feet

Thank You, Thank You, Thank You
For making me feel like I am someone
I wish I had better words to express my gratitude
For the love of the Father and Son

Written by Anonymous Sinner

I AM AN ANONYMOUS SINNER IN RECOVERY, AND I USED TO BE AN ADDICT! On June 6, 2006, I celebrated my first step in living drug- and alcohol-free. For that, I can only thank God.

I already have firsthand knowledge of life with addictions, and now I'm studying and writing this book so that I can help others who are struggling with what I overcame through Christ and treatment.

I truly believe that through Christ all things are possible and that in order to get what we need, we must first realize and admit that we need it. Then we must put our faith in God and trust that He will guide us to the people and places that we need in order to receive what we need through the Christ in others. You never know who or what God will use to bless you.

Once you receive your blessing, you should be a blessing to others. This book is my way of trying to give back some of what I've received through Christ.

ABOUT THE AUTHOR

The author, known as Anonymous Sinner, was born and raised in St. Louis, Missouri, in March 1964. He lived in a household with both parents and nine other siblings. His two oldest siblings were boys, one of which would die from a brain tumor and the other murdered years later before the Anonymous Sinner's seventeenth birthday, just shortly after a disagreement that they had before his brother walked away and out of the house.

The murder of this brother had a deep impact on his life as he knew he would never have a chance to apologize for the disagreement they had earlier. He also knew he was wrong and his older brother was right but decided to just walk away instead of arguing.

This led him deeper into an addiction that started at the age of twelve, while trying to find a place to fit in because he did not feel like his dad cared enough about him to pay him enough attention. He was blessed enough as a child to have a mother who would take him to church and teach him about a savior called Jesus who loved him so much that He died for him long before the Anonymous Sinner would even hear of this savior named Jesus. This would be a name he would need to call on later in a crucial moment in his life.

Though as a young man he strayed further and further from church, he would from time to time say a vague prayer or give thanks for another chance to try to do something right. On 6-6-06, while smoking crack and having chest pains in a vacant building he was living in, he got serious, fell to his knees, and called on Jesus, and Jesus showed up.

As the years have gone by, he has learned to love himself more. He is also still learning how to use his free will to stop and rethink about how to react to some of his thoughts. He does this with the understanding that not all days would be good days but that no matter what situation occurs there will never be a day when just one hit won't hurt.

He does not go to church every Sunday because he is a super saint with everything figured out; he goes to church because he has figured out that he is a sinner in recovery who has been influenced by the words of men, and he needs more influence in his life from the words of God.

CPSIA information can be obtained
at www.ICGtesting.com
Printed in the USA
FFOW04n0900030518
46438625-48317FF